The Mother Load

The Mother Load

Nancy Crochiere

NEVER
THE
LESS
Press

www.neverthelesspress.com

First edition 2014
Printed in the United States of America

ISBN-13: 978-0615915968
ISBN-10: 0615915965

In memory of my mom, whose laughter
is always with me

Contents

Acknowledgments

The Daily News of Newburyport, Massachusetts, published my columns from late 1997 to early 2011, and I thank them for allowing me to reprint a selection of them. For almost that entire time, my editor was Sonya Vartabedian, whose encouragement was unflagging and whose gentle editorial queries ("Did you maybe fall asleep in the middle of that sentence?") were always spot-on. I'm also grateful for the support of Katie Lovett of *The Daily News*, and Christine Gillette, who was editor of *The Eagle-Tribune* during the years when my column ran in that paper.

My women's book group has provided unflagging support since 1995. In between eating bean dip and figuring out who actually has read this month's book, we nurture members' goals and aspirations and have each other's back in good times and bad. In addition, some of these friends offered specific skills and guidance: Mary Cullen pulled me kicking and screaming into the world of social networking; Joan Atkinson offered personal coaching to help me realize my writing goals; and Beth Eames has shared encouragement and a sharp editorial eye.

My friends at The First Religious Society, Unitarian-Universalist Church in Newburyport, Massachusetts, have also been a great source of encouragement. Maxine Steeves first gave me the idea of publishing a collection some years ago, and Marj Babcock was never going to give me a minute's peace at coffee hour until I finished it. I thank them for giving the best possible meaning to the phrase "to nudge."

In the early years of writing the column, my BFF Susan Beauchamp commented on drafts when I was not yet brave enough to submit them for publication without a second set of eyes. Also, the editorial advice and consistent prodding ("Will you just publish that book so I don't have to buy holiday gifts?") of my publishing colleague, Naomi Friedman, has helped keep me motivated.

My eternal gratitude goes to Robin Mouat for the cover and interior design, to Sullivan Studios for the photos, and to Caryl Sindoni for making sure I looked my best in them. And heartfelt thanks to Tracy Plass, Susan Shaw-Meadow, Rhona Robbin, and the aforementioned book group for convincing me that a goofy, not glamorous cover photo works best on a humor book. (Darn.)

Finally, I need to thank my husband Paul and daughters Danielle and Rebecca for being such jolly good sports about having their family life chronicled in the newspaper for 15 years. Apart from Danielle's denial that she ever braked to avoid hitting a fuzzy caterpillar (she did), and Becca's request that I not write about carving our Halloween pumpkins on Christmas Eve (I did write about it), they never uttered a peep of protest. They have always been my biggest supporters and I remain their biggest fan.

Note

I've organized these columns by theme rather than chronology, so in one column my children may be ages 5 and 9, while in the next they are 18 and 22. (Interestingly, that's how it seemed to happen in life, too.) Be assured that they are always the same two children and I've usually provided indications of their age; however if you are momentarily disoriented in moving from one piece to the next, feel free to blame them for growing up so fast. I know I do.

PART 1

Married Life: Sleeping with the Enemy

I'll Never Lube This Way Again

I tried to warn my husband that he and his car were getting a reputation.

"I beg your pardon?" he said.

"You're an oil-change tramp," I explained as I paged through our car receipts. "Look at this—it's someplace different every time: Fast Lube, Zippy Oil Change, Quickie Lube, the Don't-Ask-Don't-Tell Garage."

He had to admit I was right. The truth is that my husband doesn't care where he gets his lube job. In fact, he will acknowledge, the more anonymous the encounter, the better.

I don't subscribe to this philosophy. I believe in establishing a long-term relationship with my garage. I want them to call me when I'm overdue to have my fluids replaced, check out my headlights without being asked, put a little sticker on my windshield telling me when I'll see them again.

Oh, I tried the anonymous route. It didn't work for me.

The people at Zippy Change didn't understand my needs at all. They hustled me in and out without even asking my name. The whole thing was over in 10 minutes. "Really?" I wondered. "Is that it? I've had longer interactions with my cash machine!" They looked puzzled.

Things were no better at Real-Cheap-and-Easy Lube, only there, they wanted to talk filth to me. I sat in their waiting room for barely two minutes before one of them approached me, holding a small, dingy object.

"This is really dirty," he said. "Do you want to replace it?"

I stared at the car part. Frankly, it looked no dirtier than anything else I'd glimpsed under a hood. How, I wondered, could I even be sure it came from my car? For all I knew, it was part of their coffeemaker. But the mechanic was waiting for a response, so I did the only thing I could: I faked it.

"Go for it," I smiled weakly.

I had nightmares about this encounter for weeks. I'm fairly certain the mechanic went out back and high-fived his buddies, chortling loudly over the woman who just authorized $40 of repairs to a cup holder.

After that experience, I'd had it with "quickies." I wanted a garage I could commit to—someplace where they would keep my phone number on file, where they would give me a key ring with their name on it.

It took several tries, but I finally found the perfect repair place. They couldn't take me right away. I needed to make an appointment. "Playing hard-to-get," I sighed. "I love that in a garage."

More importantly, the mechanics there seemed willing to speak my language. They only asked me questions I could answer, like "Do you need a ride home?" or "Would you like a free litter bag?"

Still, it wasn't until my car started making an unusual noise that I knew for certain that this was the place for me.

"What kind of noise?" inquired the mechanic.

"Bad," I whimpered.

He handed me a *National Enquirer* and took my car keys. Twenty minutes later, he returned.

"I'm afraid that the pressure regulator is limiting the pressure to the fuel injection system," he said.

I looked at the mechanic for a long time before I spoke. "I was an

English major," was all I could finally muster.

"Oh, right," he nodded. He sized me up and then thought for several minutes, choosing his words carefully.

Finally, he said: "Mr. Car is sick."

I sighed, overcome by the depth of my understanding.

"But, I think," the mechanic finished, "we can make him better."

"Oh, thank you," I cried. That was the moment I knew I had found the garage of my dreams.

It's been several years since I gave myself to this garage, and the relationship has proved mutually satisfying. I pay them for their services and they provide me with gossipy reading material and a promise never to talk about fuel-injection systems, or anything else that might kill my mood.

My husband, on the other hand, continues to be cavalier about his oil changes, getting his car serviced wherever he pulls off the road. It works for him. He's even found some places that will flush his cooling system and vacuum his interior.

"Sure," I reply. "But will they respect you in the morning?"

I'm Trying Hard to Be Green,
but It's Making Me Blue

Robert Frost once wondered whether the world would end in fire or ice. Many people have wondered the same thing about my marriage.

Each year as the cold weather sets in, my husband and I engage in a complicated dance centered around the house thermostat.

A casual observer might assume that it is some kind of ritual mating dance—that is, until they notice it is not all that friendly.

It begins like this: Every morning, I waltz downstairs and give the thermostat a quick flick-of-the-wrist to change the temperature from its current "arctic wasteland" setting to one that could actually support human life—say, 68 degrees.

Approximately fifteen minutes later, just as my toes have regained some feeling and my lips have lost their corpse-like purple tinge, my husband silently glides into the room and moves the thermostat back to 64.

I sashay left, slip back into the living room, and nudge it up to 70. He promenades right, sees what I have done, and changes it to 62.

Then comes the do-si-do. Glaring intently, I stroll around him and crank the thermostat to a setting that I like to call "This House is Toast."

Returning my glare, he moves to my left and spins the dial back to the "Even Inuits Wouldn't Live Here" zone.

I won't describe the rest of the choreography, but it's not pretty. Let's just say that we are unlikely to be recruited for "Dancing with the Stars" this season. We would have a better shot auditioning for "Friday Night Smackdown."

My husband and I have been dancing around the issue of "comfort zones" for most of our marriage. He is a man who doesn't own a sweater, thinks a fun vacation is sea kayaking in Alaska, and believes any activity can be improved by adding ice cubes. I, on the other hand, buy my sweaters so they can be layered. I wear turtlenecks for so much of the year that my friends compete for the first Adam's apple sighting of the spring. The words "global warming" give me a warm, fuzzy feeling inside.

Lately, however, our comfort-zone dance has become trickier, because my husband started playing the "green" card—that is, using my guilt about conserving energy to keep me from touching the thermostat.

He's right, of course: it is good to be green. Although I suspect in my husband's case, he is less worried about our dwindling natural resources than the dwindling green stuff in our checking account, which he constantly imagines is flying out our poorly insulated windows.

But it is also, in the words of a famous frog, not easy being green— especially when parts of you are turning blue. And wrapping yourself in quilts can only get you so far when the interior of your house is the temperature of downtown Fargo.

And so, our dancing continues.

There is also a night-time version. It begins after my husband turns down the heat each night, choosing a temperature so low that I check my toothbrush each morning for frost.

My part in this nocturnal dance is simple. I don't move. Indeed, I can't move after slipping under the enormous stack of blankets, quilts, afghans, and comforters piled on my side of the bed. Trust me—the lost city of Pompeii was not buried under as many layers as I have covering me on a December night.

My husband's part in the dance is more complicated. As the room temperature drops, he spends several hours rolling back and forth, grabbing one layer after another from my stack of blankets. This continues until about 3 a.m., when I lean over and threaten his manhood.

That's the end of the dance—at least until morning, when we start all over again.

You see, that's the good thing about dancing—and even the occasional marital smackdown: at least it keeps you warm.

And as long as I'm warm, I won't be blue.

Free Time Can Be Dangerous for Couples

Most people I know complain that they don't have enough leisure time. But I'm here to tell you that free time can be a dangerous thing, especially for couples.

I've seen too much leisure time actually destroy marriages.

In my experience, couples rarely agree on how to spend their free hours. My ideal leisure-time activity goes something like this: I'm lying on the beach while someone—and I'm not all that particular about who, as long as he bears a remarkable resemblance to George Clooney—rubs coconut oil on my back.

For some reason, my husband doesn't support me in this vision. His idea of how I should spend my free time is helping him paint the shed. We have agreed to disagree on this.

But even absent my George Clooney fantasy, my husband and I consistently clash over the issue of recreational time. He scoffs that I while away my free hours reading "chick books," which I then discuss with my women's book group. He's convinced that this group actually spends 90 percent of its meeting time discussing men and their failings. This is not true at all. We spend, at most, 70 percent of the evening on this. We need some time to eat cheesecake.

I counter that my husband devotes his free time to making people dislike him. He achieves this by sitting on our town's zoning board. Here, he alternately tells people that no, they cannot build a deck over their neighbor's patio, and yes, they do have to take down that four-story garage, because such structures do not conform to zoning laws. These decisions make him so popular that after the meetings, applicants often hang around the parking lot to thank him personally.

I asked him once why he chooses to spend his time in this way. He told me that he meets a lot of new people.

"So do the state troopers giving out speeding tickets on Route 495," I observed. "And they make just as many friends."

He shrugged. "Someone has to do it."

I guess. Someone also has to pick up the trash along the highway, but generally these people aren't spending free time—they're doing hard time.

In our family, disagreements over free time get especially testy around the subject of vacations. My husband's definition of a successful vacation is one in which family members rise at daybreak, pack in as much nonstop "fun" as possible before nightfall, and finally stumble back to the hotel room looking like survivors of the Donner Party Expedition.

In contrast, my ideal vacation involves floating in a pool, holding one of those drinks with a little pink umbrella.

While I accuse him of planning vacations that resemble a week at boot camp, he counters that my idea of a vacation is virtually indistinguishable from being comatose.

Luckily, we don't have to deal with these conflicts often. By limiting our vacations to one per year, we effectively contain the damage and can resume our post-vacation lives with a minimum of professional counseling.

Observe how good we've become at respecting each other's choices: right now, my husband is busily poring through travel guides, making a list of 27 activities that we can aspire to complete in our week-long trip. I am busily ignoring him.

Ever the planner, he reminds me, "Someone's got to do this."

I suppose. We each have our roles. I would assert, though, that someone also has to support the coconut oil industry, and I am personally willing to shoulder that responsibility.

Men Lack Shopping Genes

Regardless of how non-sexist your relationship is—I don't care if he gets pedicures and she does all the channel-surfing—I'll guarantee that everything breaks down by gender when it comes to shopping.

It's the retail experience that irrevocably divides the sexes. Modern research has shown that somewhere on the female X-chromosome is a tiny gene that, when magnified 10,000 times, reveals a logo for the Gap or Crate & Barrel. Men have no such gene.

My husband breaks into hives anywhere within parking distance of a mall. He is convinced that the music of Michael Bolton played over department store speakers can sterilize a healthy man at 500 yards.

The result is that he avoids any shopping experience that doesn't involve purchasing mulch or new windshield wipers. And that has created a problem for our marriage because he doesn't know what anything costs. He thinks jeans still cost what they did during the Carter administration.

His ideas about our children's clothing needs are even more out-of-touch. "Shoes!" he'll rail at our daughter's newest purchase. "But you already have a pair of shoes!" This attitude has not won him fans among the pre-teen set.

No, it's been clear to me for some time that the only way to educate my husband on the realities of the retail world was to drag him, kicking and screaming, into his own personal heart of darkness: a suburban shopping mall.

The question was, how?

I first tried bribery. I waved a Victoria's Secret catalog in his face.

"Look what they have at the mall," I enticed.

He scoffed. "No way. They don't have anything like that at the mall." But I could tell I had his attention.

Next, I tried proven psychological techniques to desensitize him to the shopping experience. While we drove to the mall, I asked him to visualize himself someplace comfortable and safe: watching a Patriots game on TV, for example. To get him out of the car, I told him to imagine that he was just getting up to fill his popcorn bowl.

As we entered the mall, throngs of people crisscrossed in front of us. I could feel my husband pull back. "Too many players on the field," he said, shaking his head.

I knew I had to get him into a store fast. Out of the corner of my eye, I could see him peeling off layers of clothes. The mall sweats had begun.

"Look," I said, pointing to a small, non-threatening shop. "I think I see some mulch in there."

He wasn't biting. "This is a bath and body lotion shop."

"No, really," I assured him. "I'm pretty sure I see some wiper fluid in the back…" I turned just in time to catch a glimpse of his head disappearing through the crowd. He was gone.

In my heart, I know the problem is not my husband. It's his genes. Recently the media has been running stories about how holiday shopping raises men's stress levels. Apparently, studies show that the blood pressure of a man while shopping is as high as that of a fighter pilot going into combat duty or a police officer entering a dangerous situation.

But I still hold out hope for the future. After all, they're doing great things these days with gene replacement therapy.

No One Make a Move! Advice on Relocating without Pain

Moving is like childbirth. If you're not careful, you can easily forget what a truly horrible experience it is and consider repeating it in a couple years.

My advice: Don't do it. Take it from someone who's been there. The breathing didn't help. There was no time for drugs—everything went too fast. They told me not to push, but I couldn't help it. And this was just getting the piano into my living room.

Nothing can prepare you for the pain of a move. (The Welcome Wagon people prefer the word "discomfort," but I won't lie to you.) Moving is one of life's most traumatic events; it is rated high on the stress scale—somewhere between filing for bankruptcy and adopting a rescue porcupine.

Despite this, no one offers "pre-moving" classes. No one offered me explicit drawings of how the futon would be delivered through my attic crawl space. There was no advice on how chanting words like "hut, hut, hee" could help me stuff the guinea pig cage into the station wagon.

So, while the trauma is still fresh in my mind, I'm offering a short course for the novice mover. Let me be your coach. Put on some comfy clothes, pull up a pillow, and I'll help you prepare for the hard labor of moving. Here are a few helpful hints:

First, before you can even consider a move, you must save every box that enters your house for approximately 12 years. I know, I know, you don't have room to store all this stuff—that's why you're moving, dummy.

Second, don't let children pack their own belongings. Sure, making them take responsibility for their possessions seems like a real good idea at first. That is, until you try to unpack and find, on the bottom of one soggy carton, what was once a box of popsicles.

Third, don't let the organized person do the packing. In every household, there is an organizer. If this person does the packing, by moving day you will have no more than 2½ meticulously packed boxes and a marital crisis that even Dr. Phil won't touch.

On the other hand, don't let the efficient person do the packing, either. In our family, this is my husband. Want something done fast? Call my husband. A week before our move, he packed the kitchen. Everything. For seven long days, I could find neither a crumb to eat nor a utensil to stab him with.

As a result, on our third day of importing breakfast from Dunkin Donuts, when my daughter spilled her bottle of lemonade all over the kitchen floor, we were unable to locate a single paper towel, dish towel, or napkin. Eventually, using Yankee ingenuity, we wiped the floor with a box of Kotex Light Day Pads. Happily, I can report that they are just as absorbent as they claim.

So, who should do the packing? If possible, no one. My advice to you: Don't move. It's far worse than you can imagine. Stay where you are. Build a deck. Finish the basement. Park an RV in your front yard. Do anything you can to distract yourselves from the idea of relocating.

Adopt a porcupine.

PART 2

Travel Is Clearly Not My Bag

Take a Hike, but Don't Invite Me

My husband recently snapped a great photo of our children, looking wind-swept and ruddy, on top of Mount Washington, where he led us all on a hike.

I do not appear in this photo. At the time the photo was taken, I was on my cell phone, trying to dial the spousal abuse hotline. With my other hand, I was clinging to a rock.

My husband has long wanted our family to hike Mount Washington—the highest peak in the Northeast. In his youth, he and his brothers often climbed this mountain. Apparently, in his family, this was considered jolly good fun.

Personally, I considered it jolly good grounds for divorce. In fact, after the hike, it took an obscenely expensive dinner and days of unwinding in a hot tub before I would stop muttering about "division of assets."

I'll admit I was at fault for agreeing to this adventure in the first place. My mistake was lending my husband a copy of Bill Bryson's *A Walk in the Woods*, about hiking the Appalachian Trial. (Note to self: No more books for husband.) In retrospect, I'm just glad I didn't lend him my copy of *Into Thin Air*, about climbing Mount Everest, or *Endurance*, about crossing Antarctica.

In my enthusiasm for Bryson's book, it's *possible* I suggested that hiking some local mountains *might* be fun someday. I meant this in the same vein as "doing a triathlon might be fun someday" or "climbing a live volcano could be interesting someday." In such cases, he should understand that "someday" means "perhaps with your next wife."

But I'll also admit that I—madly, vainly, stupidly—thought I was up to it. After all, I had been doing step aerobics classes for years. Why, I figured that I must have climbed a dozen Mount Washingtons by now!

And if all that weren't reassuring enough, we were bringing our 8-year-old. Surely I had more endurance than a third-grader! I envisioned myself heroically carrying my wilted child through the last leg of the journey, the picture of maternal strength and protectiveness.

In reality, I never even caught sight of the third-grader. She was too busy competing for the lead spot with her sister, a 13-year-old who had painted her nails before the hike and carried three hairbrushes in her backpack. My humiliation was complete.

Luckily for me, my older daughter brought along a 13-year-old friend with a lot of experience babysitting. Katie generously hung back, offering me a hand over rough terrain, encouraging me with phrases like, "Easy does it" and "Good job!" When I whimpered, she patted my head and fed me trail mix.

There was further mortification. Near the top of our climb, I rested for a moment in a dried-up stream bed. Apparently, though, it only looked dry. The sagging of my soaked shorts during the remainder of the hike gave new meaning to my job of "holding up the rear."

Two hours later, as that rear collapsed in a heap at the base of the mountain, my husband made the mistake of jauntily asking, "Now, wasn't that the most fun you've ever had?"

I told him, with a great deal of earnestness, that it was certainly the most fun *he* could expect to have on this vacation.

Of course, the whole mountain-climbing experience is much like childbirth, in that you quickly forget the pain. Somehow, within a few days, my husband had convinced us all that a second hike, around the "foothills" of Mount Washington, would be fun. He referred to a map in the guidebook showing that the trail was relatively flat.

Hours later, as I clung from the side of a cliff with my family hovering above me and Katie calling down "You can do it!" I cross-examined my husband on his definition of the word "flat."

"It looked flat on paper," he shrugged.

"Paper is two-dimensional," I yelled. "Everything looks flat on paper!"

He suggested that if I couldn't make it up in half an hour, they would airlift some trail mix to me.

I won't delve into the details of the marital discussion that followed that hike. Suffice it to say, we've redefined our notion of "family fun" to exclude activities that lead to separate hotel rooms for the parents. Our next trip, we have all agreed, will involve nothing more strenuous than some beach time and a relaxing whale watch.

(Note to self: Hide copy of *Moby Dick*.)

The Plane Truth: Confessions
of a Nervous Flier

I'm sitting at the boarding gate for my flight, staring at my backpack.

Airport security has just made an announcement over the loud-speaker: "We are on Orange Alert, so please watch your baggage closely. Report immediately any suspicious baggage activity."

So, I'm doing as directed. I'm not sure what activity might be suspicious for a backpack, but if mine makes a move, I'm all over it.

"Don't even think about it, buster," I whisper.

Apparently, orange is a fairly serious color for a danger alert. I was hoping that orange might simply be a nice color for alerts in autumn, but no. I checked it on my smartphone. Orange, I learn, means that "for all domestic and international flights, the threat level is high."

"Way too much information," I tell my smartphone and shut it off.

Then I look around me, wondering how many people have just witnessed me twice talking to inanimate objects.

It's no secret that I'm not at my best on airplanes.

Flight attendants see me coming, even before I actually board the aircraft. I'm the one tapping on the plane exterior to confirm its sturdiness; examining the seal around the doorway hatch; peering into the cockpit to see if the pilot and co-pilot look alert and well rested.

I always choose a window seat and keep my eyes trained on the wing. During the flight, nothing—not even the lure of complimentary pretzels—will tear my gaze from its flaps and other moving parts. My only regret is that I have but one wing to watch for my flight crew.

My husband has occasionally suggested that the flight crew doesn't really need my help. I'm not so sure. I once read about a little old lady who saw a piece of wing fall off the plane and reported it to the pilot, allowing him to land the plane safely. I'm convinced that this kind of heads-up attitude in life is what allows one to become a little old lady in the first place.

Despite his blasé attitude about air safety, I generally prefer to fly with my husband, as I can grab him during a bumpy ride without risking a restraining order. Whether the plane is actually spiraling down in a death spin or simply banking a turn before landing—and these things are often indistinguishable to me—at least I am on a first name basis with the person I'm digging my nails into.

For this flight, though, I am alone, and as I continue to watch my backpack for any unexpected activity, I reflect again that airports today are giving us way too much information. For example:

An hour ago, our flight was delayed and the airline informed us they were changing our plane because a light had burned out—specifically, the light that helps pilots avoid runway collisions. Now, personally, I didn't need to know that the responsibility for avoiding runway collisions rests on one light, and that this light can burn out. All they needed to tell me is that we're changing planes because the new plane is a prettier color. I'm good with that.

Second, they need to scrap the TVs at the gates. The news show playing on the overhead TV is doing a feature on the increasing incidence of deep-vein thrombosis—potentially fatal blood clots—from long flights in cramped conditions. Now, thanks to that bulletin, I can obsess in a whole new way about how flying can kill me. In order to reduce my blood clot risk on today's flight, I decide to do a little Tai Chi in the aisle. I expect that I will be offered a great many packages of free pretzels—and not just from the flight attendants—if I agree to resume my seat.

Finally, as a rule, the crew should keep it to themselves if something during the flight seems out-of-the-ordinary. They need to avoid the kind of off-hand comment that causes people to tune their headphones to the religious channels. No such luck on this flight. Not long after take-off, when the plane takes a sudden dip and hits some heavy turbulence, the flight attendant steadies herself and remarks, "Wow! What was that? I've never felt anything like that before!"

I want to remind her that when someone's stomach is already in her throat, there's nowhere for the pretzels to go but up.

Instead, I keep a tight hold on my thoughts and stomach content and order a double gin and tonic.

I figure that now, at least, if I see my backpack moving, I'll have a good idea why.

The French Have a Different Word for Everything!

There is some loose talk in my family that we may try vacationing in Paris this summer. Such talk makes me nervous.

It's not that I worry about too many breakfasts of croissants and creamy French butter. After all, this is why God invented elastic waistbands.

Nor do I fear that my daughters will want to shop in the exclusive Paris boutiques, further refining their already pricey idea of fashion. I don't think it can get much pricier.

No, I'm nervous for one reason only: My family thinks I can speak French.

Now, in their defense, they have good reason to believe this: I told them I could.

And for years, they have had no reason to doubt me because (1) I was their wife/mother, and (2) we didn't happen to be in France.

My family believes that I speak fluent French because, as a college student, I studied for a semester in Paris. In truth, though, I was an English major who bluffed her way into a semester abroad by relying heavily on a French-English dictionary.

Oh, sure, I eventually picked up some knowledge of the language while in Paris. I learned how to find a restroom, order my Big Mac with no mustard and ketchup, and pretend I wasn't American. "I'm just a Canadian who likes Big Macs, eh?"

But I'm not sure much of it has stayed with me.

My husband remembers a few phrases from his high school French. For example, he definitely will be our "go-to" guy should anyone happen to ask, "Does Pierre have a blue pen?" He instinctively will know to reply, "Yes, Pierre has a blue pen." Only sometimes he still gets a word wrong, and it comes out, "Yes, Pierre has a blue spleen," or "Yes, Pierre is dating his pen." You're never quite sure.

I have this recurring nightmare that I will try to buy something from a Parisian bakery and the conversation (in French) will go something like this:

Baker: Good morning! How are you?

Me: Feelings is fine tomorrow, thank you. May I feel you?

Baker (a bit miffed): Would you like to buy something?

Me: Yes, round is something I would like. And something green.

Baker: We are all out of green pastries today; would you like to choose another color?

Me: Perhaps something with the flavor of hamster?

At this point in my dream, the baker chases me out the door with a baguette.

Of course, my anxiety about vacationing in France is not limited to speaking the language. I can get nervous about almost any aspect of the trip. Here, in no particular order, are my top fears:

1. During our middle-of-the-night layover in Iceland, the Ice people (or whatever they call themselves...Icicles?) will experience an airline strike, stranding us for two weeks in Reykjavik, a place I can barely pronounce, never mind spell.

2. Once in Paris, a man on the subway will say something rude, and I will smile and reply in mangled French, "Thank you, I enjoy prairie dogs, too."

3. Parisian men will hassle my teenage daughters... and not me.

4. My husband will wake us before daybreak so that we can climb the Eiffel Tower before the crowds of tourists arrive. (Please note: the anxiety-producing phrase here is not "before daybreak," but "climb.")

5. The house we are staying in will have a plumbing problem and I'll call a gynecologist.

6. I will misread the menu at a restaurant and be unable to eat what I have ordered because I am pretty sure my entree is a distant relation of our pet, Bun-Bun.

7. After misinterpreting a highway "yield" sign as "drive fast," we will be pulled over by a police officer and my husband will try to speak French. Luckily, the officer's name is Pierre and he does have a blue pen, which he uses to write up the citation.

My list goes on, but in spite of all these fears, I am looking forward to our trip. I keep telling my family, "Allons-y!," which I'm pretty sure means "Let's go!" although it might mean "How silly we are!"

I suppose that works, too.

A Letter to the President of France with a Few Small Suggestions

Dear Mr. President:

Since my family and I were just vacationing in France, I hope you don't mind if I offer a few suggestions on ways you might make your country more welcoming for Americans. Because I'm sure that is high on your list of priorities, right after saving the euro and finding a replacement for Jerry Lewis.

Here are my observations:

1. You have no decaffeinated Diet Coke. No wonder your people drive so fast! Also, this does a lot to explain how quickly you speak.

2. You drink coffee in cups the size of a shot glass. In the U.S., we don't call that coffee—we call it "a free sample." Coffee is the drink that comes in enormous cups called "Big Gulps" ("Les Gulps Grandes," in your language). We carry these cups around all morning while we work or drive the kids to school. When we're done, we go to Starbucks or Dunkin Donuts and buy another.

3. Toilets must have seats. I'm pretty sure this is a minimum requirement for membership in NATO.

4. Your road signs are all in French! This is all well and good for you, but—just a suggestion here—perhaps we should think of

others before ourselves? After all, you folks already know where Marseilles is.

5. You eat cute animals. We put bunnies and ducks in our children's Easter baskets; you put them in your children's stews. Perhaps you could consider switching to chicken, fish or Black Angus cattle? These animals are patently not cute.

6. Your rental cars have no cup holders. Puh-leeze!

7. I've noticed that you've added some English words to your lexicon, like "cool," "le weekend," and "le parking." Great! I'd like it if you would add a few more words of English. For example, the following would have been a big help to me:

"Am I on the road to Lyons AGAIN?

"Did my dinner entrée once have a name?"

"I've just used the wrong adapter for my hairdryer and blown out the electricity on 3 floors of your hotel."

It's possible that these examples may require more than one word. I'm sure you can figure it out.

8. I know you are fond of the metric system, but you may want to think about substituting our mile for your kilometer. Ours is bigger. Plus, it makes places seem a lot closer.

9. My teenage daughters thought some of your French boys were cute, but have just two words for them: Right Guard.

10. The Eiffel Tower is nice, but really—does it need to be that tall? And if the elevators must contain windows, can they at least include little air-sick bags for nervous tourists? Even worse, your observation deck at the very top seems to "sway" a little. Personally, I'm not fond of "sway" at 320 meters.

11. The Louvre was fabulous and ever so educational for our family. However, could some of the statues be dressed more modestly? Even a Speedo would help.

I hope you don't take offense at my pointing out these differences in our cultures. Please feel free to write back and give me your suggestions for the United States. I'll warn you in advance, though, that we can't make Caramel Frapaccinos any smaller than they are.

A bientot!
Nancy

My Date with Airport Security (or How I Was Nearly Mistaken for a Terrorist)

To appreciate this story, you first have to understand that I am a girl scout.

I obey rules. I don't jay-walk. I take a multi-vitamin. I floss my teeth daily. I recycle, always wear a seatbelt, and never leave the dryer running when I leave the house. I vote in every election. I tip the pizza delivery boy. I always return my shopping cart to the corral.

So, characteristically, before I took a flight to Denmark last week to visit my daughter who is studying there, I went onto the Transportation Security Administration website and reviewed the list of items that I couldn't bring on board the plane.

For the average traveler, the list seems pretty funny. It includes things like swords, meat cleavers, ice picks, spear guns, nunchuks, and cattle prods. Dynamite, hand grenades, and tear gas are also prohibited, just in case you were wondering. What kind of an idiot, I chuckled to myself, would try to pass through security with a blow torch?

As it turns out, there are more kinds of idiots than I realized.

When the big day came and I moved toward the airport security checkpoint, I was in prime girl-scout mode. I had my little Ziploc baggie containing a 4-ounce bottle of shampoo and even my contact lens case—with about 5 drops of solution—available for full inspection. I had already taken off my shoes, removed my laptop, and placed my jacket and polar fleece on the conveyer belt. I didn't beep when I went through the little archway. I was so proud.

That is, until I noticed that my backpack was apparently stuck in the X-ray machine. I wasn't really surprised by this—I had crammed an awful lot of stuff into that backpack. It was huge. I was, however, surprised when, instead of trying to jimmy it out, the woman reading the monitor called to one of her colleagues and they both stood there, watching the screen.

I suddenly began to consider how I might have screwed up. Could the inside of the thin mints I was bringing to my daughter count as a "cream"? What about the liquid-like center of Lindt truffles? Was I about to be detained for my chocolate condition?

"Ma'am," said the security guard, "we're seeing something suspicious in your bag. Are you by any chance carrying a Leatherman?

"A leather *man*?" I repeated, puzzled.

"Yes," said the security guard, clearly impatient. "Do you have one in your bag?"

"I don't think so," I whispered, still trying desperately to think what a leather man might be. A Walkman in a leather case? An anatomically correct blow-up doll in cowhide?

Convinced that what the TSA agents were seeing was my camera, its charger, or the cable cord for my computer, I helpfully emptied the bag and identified each of these objects for the security guard. (He already seemed to know what they were.) Then I showed him the inside of the bag. See, nothing up my sleeve.

That's when the security guy fished around in the depths of the backpack and pulled out what appeared to me to be some kind of instrument of torture. He methodically starting flipping open its wire-cutter, saw tools, and long and very sharp-looking straight blades.

"Let me guess," I whispered. "That would be a Leatherman."

I had never seen one before in my life. However, at this point, I remembered that my husband had taken the backpack hiking a few weeks earlier; clearly, he must have left this Mother-of-all-Swiss-Army-Knives in the bottom of the bag. That story sounded pretty lame, even to me, but it was all I had.

The guard looked me up and down. He must have sensed the whole girl-scout thing because he let me go with just a full-body wanding; however, not before informing me that if the knife blade had been one inch bigger, he would have had to call the State Police.

I nodded, trying to look sufficiently chastened, and headed for the lounge. I had never been much of an airport drinker, but this seemed like a good time to start.

As I sat at the bar, I decided that being a girl scout does have its advantages. At the very least, no one will ever mistake you for a terrorist.

And just to be sure, before I boarded the plane, I flossed.

Defining "Vacation" Is Key to Enjoying It

A few weeks ago, my husband and I decided to try a brief vacation in Maine—a 4-day weekend without kids. I say "try" because historically, the two of us have had trouble defining "vacation" in precisely the same way.

Picture this scene in our living room the evening before the trip. My husband is scouring several travel books to determine the best places in Acadia National Park to hike, bike, and kayak. Across the room from him, I am searching the internet for the best places near Acadia to shop and enjoy really fancy dinners.

Already you sense the underlying tension here.

We each understand that we operate within certain boundaries. He knows that he is prohibited from choosing any hike whose description includes the words "strenuous," "challenging," "hypothermia," "sheer drop," or "reported fatalities."

I, in turn, must refrain from choosing any restaurant whose online reviews include the word "pricey." I also need to avoid phrases like "lemon truffle risotto," "red pepper bisque," or "roulade of veal with lobster and fennel stuffing served with an orange buerre blanc and a demi-glace drizzle," all of which he sees as just code words for "pricey."

Of course, this list is not comprehensive; there are other vacation phrases on which we tend to disagree. For example, I feel any vacation worth its salt should include key words like "heated pool," "private

Jacuzzi," "good book," "dry Chardonnay," and "George Clooney movie." In contrast, his favorite phrases are "frequent moose sightings," "no crowds," "breakfast included," and "free ice."

My husband believes the words I employ most on vacation are, "Put it on my Visa," but this is only partly true. Actually, my favorite vacation phrase is, "Put it *all* on my Visa." It's a subtle distinction, but meaningful, I feel.

However, the one vacation word on which we differ most is "relaxing."

My husband is an exercise enthusiast. He never seems to tire. After a morning spent riding our bikes to the top of a mountain, he will leave me—broken and incoherent—at the hotel, while he goes out to "get some exercise." I swear that if he had been part of the Bataan Death March, he would have asked afterwards if he could go for a quick run to work up a sweat.

Now, I don't mind a little exercise on vacation—just not the kind that leaves me lifting each leg manually to climb the two small steps in the hotel lobby.

This particular trip was typical. After three days of non-stop hiking and biking, I actually asked a bellboy with luggage cart if he would give me a lift back to our room. (He thought I was joking.)

On the fourth and final day of our brief getaway, my husband rose at 6:30 and asked if I would like to accompany him on a hike.

I told him he was giving new meaning to the term "long weekend."

Wisely interpreting this response as a "no," my husband went off by himself. I slept, read my book, lounged in the hot tub, and sat by the waterfront. I wandered through the little shops in town, occasionally showing my Visa card to those store clerks who seemed eager to admire my signature.

When my husband returned from his hike several hours later, he asked if I had enjoyed my time alone.

"Yes," I admitted. "Call me crazy, but for a few hours there, it almost felt like I was on vacation."

He smiled, but I could tell he was just being polite. It was clear he had no clue what I was talking about.

People Separated by a Common Language

I thought I knew what to expect when our family went on vacation in Great Britain.

Silly me.

For one thing, I assumed we spoke the same language as these people.

Granted, the British are not like the French, who insist on having their own darn word for everything. No, the Brits are even trickier. They use the same words we use, only with completely different meanings.

To begin with, over there, things—not people—are "smart." This is true regardless of whether you're talking about shops or clothes or a new sofa. Now, as their sofas did not appear any more intelligent than mine, this emphasis on smartness seemed just a little competitive to me.

However, I noticed that when someone made a mistake—for example, when a waitress spilled my Diet Coke—she tended to mutter "Brilliant!" So, there you go: smart is good, but brilliant is bad. Are you beginning to see how tricky this is?

Another difference I learned a bit late. Apparently, in Britain, "pants" means underwear. (What we call "pants," they call "trousers.") So, as we stood in a crowd of hundreds watching the changing of the guard, and I repeatedly said to my teenaged daughter—who was wearing a cute little dress and shivering in the cool wind—that she really should have worn pants, I'm hoping the people around us were either hard-of-hearing or spoke only Hungarian.

Sometimes it just took people a few seconds to understand what we were saying. This happened after we were caught in a torrential downpour in Oxford. My daughter's flip-flops provided no traction on the wet stone streets, so inevitably, she fell and gashed open her big toe.

We ducked inside a shop and I kneeled down to examine her toe, trying to staunch the bleeding with the only thing I had available: a cash register receipt. The curious shop manager came over to ask if he could help.

"Our daughter has a bloody toe," my husband explained.

The shopkeeper paused, and for a moment I'm sure he was thinking, "We all have bleedin' toes, mate!"

But then it seemed to register and he trotted off to find us a "plaster" (Band-Aid).

A second problem arose because the downpour completely soaked my only pair of sneakers and I had brought nothing else to wear. So, I tried to buy a new pair. Only no one seemed to understand what I wanted.

"You want trainers?" asked the man behind the counter as I dripped on his floor.

I was taken aback. This sounded to me like some kind of diaper. I know I looked drenched, but really!

"No, just a pair of sneakers," I said.

"Plimsolls?" he tried again.

I hadn't realized this would be so hard. I pointed to my feet. "Tennis shoes?" I tried.

"Oh, daps!" he concluded.

"Sure, daps," I replied, having no idea what he would produce. I was beginning to feel more stupid than I had in France, which is saying a lot.

In the end, it didn't really matter what we called them—the small store had no footwear in my size. So, until we were able to dry out my sneakers, I walked around the south of England in my powder-blue bedroom slippers.

I'm sure the British have a word to describe how I looked. And I'm quite certain it is not "smart."

PART 3

Parenting with Both Hands
and a Flashlight

Easy Recipes for Summer Disaster

Most of my recipes for summer disaster require only two basic ingredients:

2 children

0 school

However, variations on these recipes are possible. You may want to substitute ingredients or add in your personal favorites, like escaping hamster, decaying camp laundry, visiting in-laws, or mating poodles. The important thing is: don't feel limited. Experiment, be creative and make these recipes your own.

Twice-cooked children with beach sand

Ingredients:

   1 middle-school aged child

   1 first-grader

   A sprinkling of playmates

   Temperatures above 90 degrees

   Broken pool filter

Directions:

   Wilt children in home for several hours or until tempers reach boiling point.

Transport to salt-water environment. Coat children with thick layer of No. 45 sunscreen. Arrange on beach towels and bake on both sides for 20 minutes.

Douse in salt water. (Children will shriek, but this is merely an instinctual reaction; they feel no pain.) Remove from water when extremities turn blue and skin is icy to the touch.

Dredge children in beach sand until they resemble Shake-and-Bake chicken.

Return children to car, preheated to 350 degrees. Apply sand-coated bodies to car upholstery until moist sand achieves consistency of wet paste.

Garnish with fries.

Yields: One breaded car interior, seven baked children and one parent, beaten.

Late-rising teen on bed of fresh linens

(Based on the James Bond Theory of Cooking: "Children who have not stirred should be shaken.")

Ingredients:

Teenager wrap (teen rolled in layers of sheet, blanket, and comforter)

Sub-zero air-conditioned bedroom

Directions:

Set timer for 8 a.m. Allow teen three hours to rise, making sure she is stirring constantly.

At 11 a.m., check for doneness by poking teen with ballpoint pen in the thickest part.

If teen has still not risen, turn off air conditioner and let bake for one additional hour. Drop water by level tablespoons onto teen's face. Place Barry Manilow CD by teen's ear and experiment with volume controls.

Replace Barry Manilow with Partridge Family.

Yields: One annoyed, but fully awake, teen.

Fried mother with scrambled brains

Ingredients:

Mother with new full-time job

Two underemployed teens

Directions:

Place mother in pressure cooker. Watch as she juggles publishing job, camp schedules, and litter-trained house rabbit. Trim fat with gym workouts. Reduce husband's stock after late work hours and marathon runs.

Divide fried mother into even thirds. Reserve one-third at home to make sure everyone gets to the orthodontist on time.

Mold one-third permanently into driver's seat of Subaru. Drive in perpetual circles from softball games to beach to shopping mall.

Place one-third on bus to work in Big City. Allow to sit quietly for one hour, or until she recalls that she left the iron on.

Recombine all ingredients. Shake vigorously until mixture can no longer find its car keys.

Remove entire concoction for one week to small Caribbean island. Rub with lotion. Ply with fruity drinks and embellish with little pink umbrellas.

Sprinkle entire summer with good humor, Top-40 radio, and a sturdy pair of flip-flops.

Yields: Semisweet memories. Serves family of four with plenty of leftovers.

Let's Talk Trash

My children are never so attached to something as when they find it in the trash.

On trash pick-up day, as they leave for school, I try to distract their attention away from the barrels lining the street.

"Look!" I say, pointing down the street in the opposite direction. "Is that an armadillo?"

"Where? Where?" yells the 5-year-old. Her knowledge of indigenous New England species is—happily—quite weak.

Unfortunately, her 9-year-old sister is less of an easy mark. She knows this trash-day ruse. Instantly she zeroes in on the barrels and identifies something she can't part with.

"Ohhhh!" she wails. "Not the laundry basket!"

The green plastic laundry basket is broken on two sides, rendering it incapable of holding anything like, say, laundry. Nevertheless, I have clearly demonstrated my lack of imagination by throwing it away.

"Mom! We can use it for forts!"

"And, like, for funny hats," says the little one, parading around with it on her head.

And so, the structurally challenged basket returns to the house for rehabilitation into a garrison or stylish headdress. I'll have to do a better job of hiding it next week.

Children are unpredictable when it comes to possessions, I've learned. One day a toy is their favorite—the next day it's sucked into that black hole we call the toy box and lost to another dimension. So many toys have vanished in my younger daughter's room that we refer to it as The Bermuda Bedroom. Things fly in but never fly out.

Yet heaven forbid that any of these long-forgotten treasures be quietly laid to rest in a trash receptacle. If the waste basket contains a ratty, one-eyed, stuffed dog hidden in a Sears bag shoved inside a shoe box and covered with three layers of dryer fuzz, my children will excavate it with more determination than archeologists digging for the lost city of Pompeii.

Not that I'm sneaky about disposing of old toys. I mean, I don't purposely cram Happy Meal prizes into old toilet paper rolls and stuff them inside crushed milk cartons under last night's chicken pie tin. I have no idea how they get there.

Okay, I lie. When it comes to deep-sixing toys, I am the queen of sneak.

Ditto with artwork, although here, young egos are at stake, so I try to be extra careful. I give each creation a respectable tour on the refrigerator before retiring it to the secret Container of No Return. If no one asks for the artwork in six months, it sleeps with the fishes.

(Goldfishes, that is. You can stuff quite a bit in those little foil-lined bags.)

Despite the cunning of my artwork-recycling system, I've run into problems. Sometimes there is just not room enough on the refrigerator for even one more piece of construction paper pasted with colored macaroni. My husband—always helpful—has proposed what seems to him like the only logical solution: get more refrigerators.

Me, I've become philosophical about my children's affinity for that-which-is-tossed. Maybe it's okay that we tend to value those things in life that we're in danger of losing. I've even tried to use this as a lesson for my children, cagily applying a bit of reverse psychology.

"Well," I tell my older daughter when she complains she has no use for her younger sibling, "then I guess I'll just have to bring her out with the trash."

My daughter glances over at her sister and advises: "Better double-bag her."

Quick, Someone Give This Woman a Hand

One night a few weeks ago, my husband made a tremendous racket outside our front door.

"Couldn't get the door open," he explained as he entered, dropping a number of bundles. "I'm not used to having only one hand."

I must have stared at him a long time because I was experiencing a revelation. Here, I realized, was yet another reason why men and women live in parallel, but completely nonintersecting, universes.

Men have two hands.

I'm pretty sure that the last time I used two hands for anything was in 1987.

That was back before my arms filled with children, diaper bags, soggy crackers, and a stuffed elephant named "Ha-Ha." In those pre-kid years I never had to waddle to the porch clutching a CVS bag between my knees. When the cantaloupe dropped out of the grocery bag, I didn't try to dribble it, soccer-style, up the walk to our house. Back then, I could open our front door without performing my Jackie Chan imitation for the neighbors. And there is no evidence that, pre-1987, I ever asked a postal employee to please just place the mail between my teeth.

But, like many women, I had to learn special adaptation techniques once I became a mother. With an infant all but soldered to my left arm, I survived by foraging for whatever food could be grasped with one hand and shoved into my mouth. For months on end, Multi-grain Cheerios were the only thing that came between me and starvation.

As the years wore on, I gained other uni-dexterous skills. I learned to drive the car with (at most) one hand. With the other, I dispensed tissues, popped straws through non-spill lids, and accepted offerings from the back seat: wads of chewed gum, melted crayons, apple cores, and the occasional gift of a soggy French fry.

As the kids grew older, things didn't get any easier—just heavier. To this day, using two hands to open a door is something I only fantasize about.

On a recent weekday, I arrived at the front door wearing a backpack and carrying two grocery bags, a basketball, a stack of library books, five pressed shirts on hangers, and some gummy worms that had sprouted fur while hibernating under the car seat. Happily, our door is now mother-accessible; all you need is the right combination of chin, shoulder, and hip, with one well-timed kick. No hands required.

I have no delusions that I'll regain the use of my limbs any time soon, but I try not to discourage others who still face years of opening milk cartons with their teeth. I recently met such a new mother working out at the gym. She had a 10-month-old at home and told me it was time to "get her body back." I smiled politely and thought, "Dream on."

In the meantime, my children are learning to do a one-handed cartwheel and I'm encouraging that skill. In fact, I'm hoping they can teach me. I can still imagine a few situations in which it might come in handy.

Our Hair-raising Adventure

A very wise man, Oscar Wilde, once said, "In this world there are only two tragedies. One is not getting what one wants, and the other is getting it."

What I don't understand is how this man, who died over a hundred years ago, understood so clearly the central irony of my life.

I'll give you a case in point: the story of my children's hair woes.

The saga began when my older daughter was just starting school. At that age, brushing the child's hair was like subjecting her to ancient Chinese water torture. (Of course, it would have helped if I had ever brushed her hair on a regular basis before she started school, but hey, it was a busy time for me, okay?)

Each morning, I was reduced to chasing her around the house. Hairbrush in hand, I hurdled sofas, skirted toddlers, leaped over open dishwashers in a single bound, and pounced from behind doorways to nab her.

It didn't end with the nabbing, of course. We then proceeded to the tantrum. Sometimes she would have one, too.

After that came the bribes—some of them involving actual cash. We usually ended with my threats to sell her to a passing carnival—which, I want to make perfectly clear, were mostly exaggerated.

When finally I touched a brush to the mass of tangles that passed for her hair, the conversations went something like this:

Wailing child: "Stop it—you're hurting me! Nobody CARES what I look like."

Mother (mumbling, her teeth clenched on an enormous pink bow): "You need to look nice for school."

Child (pinching her mother): "No one will notice. Nobody is looking at me!"

Mother (pinching child back): "No one will WANT to look at you if you look like a mess."

I have lived to regret these conversations. Because, as Mr. Wilde predicted, I got what I wanted.

A few weeks ago, as I paced the upstairs hallway, nervously counting the minutes until the school bus arrived, my now 11-year-old daughter was closeted in her bedroom, trying to get the "bumps" out of her pony-tailed hair.

If you don't have a pre-teen daughter, let me advise you: you need to view this bump-removal process from an evolutionary perspective. In the time it takes to fix bumps, glaciers can form.

"Hurry up!" I yelled at her bedroom door. "Nobody cares what you look like."

"I can't go to school like this—I look hideous," she shouted back.

"No one will notice. Nobody is looking at you that closely."

"No one will WANT to look at me if I look like a mess."

At that moment, I was hit by an odd sense of déjà vu. Where had I heard this conversation before? Not only had the child been listening all along, but I had gotten exactly what I had asked for!

Over the following weeks, I spent a lot of time puzzling over this hair business. It was important for me to understand what happened, because I had another daughter. She was in first grade—and—you guessed it—would have preferred to stick sharp things in her eye rather than have her hair brushed.

But I was confused. Which message did I want to give her?

Finally one day, as this younger daughter squirmed and moaned under my hairbrush, I took a stab at adjusting my earlier approach— the one that had succeeded so miserably (or had it failed so beautifully?) with her sister. The resulting gibberish went something like this:

"It's important to look neat, but you don't want to worry too much about your appearance. What somebody looks like shouldn't matter, but how you present yourself does. You should give a nice impression, but you don't need to fuss over every detail…"

I think there was more to it, but you get the idea.

Luckily, the 7-year-old, who has been able to call a spade a spade roughly since birth, had no time for this nonsense.

"Mom," she said, stopping the hairbrush in mid-air, "what exactly are you trying to say?"

I put down the brush.

"I have no idea," I confessed. "You're on your own."

She skipped off to meet the bus with 10 minutes to spare.

Oscar Wilde was right: there are tragedies in life. But fortunately, letting your child go to school with only one side of her hair brushed isn't one of them.

You Can Lead Your Family to Culture...

It's ironic. Before we have children, we dream of all the exciting things we will do with them. Then, once we have children, all we dream about is having 10 minutes alone in the bathroom without them.

I always dreamed of exposing my children to "culture"—a little art, some music, a bit of theatre. However, I found it easier to dream about the arts than to squeeze them into weekends spent searching for lost retainers, lifting grass stains out of uniforms, and performing science experiments with green Jell-O.

As a result, for the longest time, the only "culture" my children got was what they ingested with their yogurt. And even that had to be covered with colored sprinkles.

Waiting on the culture issue was also, I'll admit, a conscious decision. I didn't want to follow the lead of friends who had taken their preschool children to see "The Nutcracker," only to have the 3-year-old use the bathroom 7 times and the 5-year-old make rude noises with his armpit during "The Dance of the Sugar Plum Fairy."

So, I waited until my children were 8 and 12 before I took them on a PTA-sponsored trip to see "The Nutcracker" in Boston. I felt inordinately pleased with this plan; the PTA even provided a lovely coach bus for the trip.

And at first I thought my children did rather well with their introduction to ballet. Neither fell asleep, battled an overactive bladder, or made armpit noises. In fact, I left the theatre feeling pretty smug about the whole "culture" thing.

That was, until we returned home, and my younger daughter raced to the phone to tell her friend about the experience.

"We just went to see 'The Nutcracker,'" she gushed. "And guess WHAT?"

I waited expectantly for her to describe the dancing bear, the giant Christmas tree, the army of battling mice.

"You won't believe this," she continued, her little voice almost a shriek. "The bus had a *bathroom* and a *TV!*"

At that moment I realized it was possible—just possible—that I had waited a little too long on the "culture" thing.

I quickly pulled myself together for another attempt. I decided to try Culture 101: musical theatre. Within the space of a few weeks, I took the girls to see "Gypsy" and "Cabaret," at which shows they learned the word "stripper" and watched women dancing in black garters. That was the end of that; my children's clothing choices didn't need any further influence.

We took a long break from musical theatre.

That is, until just recently, when my now 14-year-old younger daughter announced that she just *had* to see the play "Wicked."

After some initial reluctance, I thought, Why not? It's about witches, right? It's about someone who has a problem being green—an issue I had felt strongly about since it was first brought to my attention by Kermit the Frog.

The trick was getting tickets. The show in Boston was sold out and ticket agencies were asking for *both* my first-born child and an amount of cash that was close to a down payment on a house. I won't say exactly where I drew the line, but I didn't have the down payment.

My past experiences with ticket scalpers hadn't been pretty. Generally, in such situations, I had searched and searched for just the right person to take full advantage of me. Then, once I had him on the line, I groveled until he was willing to add on extra fees and delivery charges. Then, and only then, was I satisfied.

This experience was no less traumatic. Though on show-day I finally scored tickets, I was told that in order to get them in time for the performance, I needed to meet up with someone named "Bobby."

"Does he have a last name?" I asked the scalper, hopefully.

"No," he replied.

Perhaps I was being unfair, but I was nervous dealing with a grown man whose only name was Bobby. He sounded like someone with a recurring role on "The Sopranos."

"If this guy introduces the word 'kneecaps,'" a co-worker offered, "I would cut and run."

In the end, however, Bobby turned out to be a 5-foot-4 delivery boy who handed over the tickets with no harm to my kneecaps. And happily, "Wicked" turned out to be a wicked good show.

So we've resumed watching musicals, but these days, more often than not, we watch them from the living room sofa. Just last week, for example, the 14-year-old invited me to watch "Rent" with her on DVD.

Now I'm the one being introduced to new terminology. I learned the word "stash" (as in "one's current supply of drugs"), and also the correct meaning of the phrase, "pole dancer," which I guess, in the past, I had always taken to mean a festively attired folk dancer from Warsaw. I was way off—on the clothing part, especially.

Sigh. It's not easy being green.

What to Expect When You're Long Past Expecting

Two weekends ago, I found myself standing for several hours in freezing weather at my 16-year-old daughter's pre-season soccer tournament. By the time her 3 games were over, I had lost sensation in several body parts—some of which I'm willing to name and some not. Happily, my husband assured me that as far as he could see, my nose was still attached to my face, which gave me hope that the other parts were hanging in there, as well.

Anyway, as I stood there wondering just what hypothermia feels like and whether severe frostbite always—or just sometimes—leads to gangrene and amputation, two other questions occurred to me. The first was: Wouldn't it be nice if hot chocolate could be taken intravenously? However, the second—and more important—question was: Why had no one prepared me for days like this?

Now granted, I didn't *have* to be standing outside, watching soccer in mid-March. I could have been home, under an afghan, reading French novels, or even sitting in the parking lot with the car heat cranked up to the setting that I like to call "August in Aruba." But no, I had chosen to be there, because I am a good parent. However, I realized that no one had ever forewarned me about the many things that are involved in good parenting. Several books tell parents-to-be "what to expect when you are expecting," but few give you the low-down on what to expect in the 20-odd years after that.

So, I started to make a mental list of all the things that I hadn't foreseen would be part of the job. The list below is based on my personal experiences, but may apply to others. For example, before you were a parent, you probably never realized that:

- Projectile vomit can go *that* far.

- You can be cajoled into reading "Goodnight Moon" so many times that you start fantasizing about popping the red balloon and making bunny stew.

- A child can wake consistently at 5 a.m. for years—until she starts school, at which point it becomes impossible to wake her any time before noon.

- Not only will you cheat at Candy Land, you will cheat in order to lose.

- You can develop a serious fear of broom handles after being beaned by a kid trying to break a piñata.

- You will be required to attend countless recitals in which your child butchers the Beethoven piece she has played flawlessly 900 times at home.

- You will not only understand the off-sides rule in soccer, but will have an almost irresistible desire to explain it to the referee, in a very loud voice.

- You will pay for years of lessons, camps, and travel sports so your child will make the high school team, only to find that, now that she's on the team, you must pay for the privilege of watching her play.

- The same child who seems to have inherited your phobia about brooms will also develop a similar aversion to closets, coat hangers, and dresser drawers.

- You may have to ride in a careening ambulance with an injured child, and although you know her broken arm is not life-threatening, you are pretty sure that the ambulance ride will kill you both. Moreover, the paramedics will give calming medication only to the child, not to you, no matter how much you beg.

- Although your child refused to eat anything other than pasta throughout her entire childhood, making the entire family into virtual vegetarians, she will return from her first semester at college and announce that "steak is yummy!"

Mine is not a complete list, of course. And I had to admit that there were also plenty of fun, exciting, and joyous aspects of parenting that I didn't foresee before embarking on the journey 20 years ago.

I resolved to think on these things—in fact, to make another list—just as soon as I could unfreeze my face to yell at the ref for that offsides call.

PART 4

Tweens and Teens—or Why Some Species Eat Their Young

Ten Reasons Why You Should Never Ski with Your Teen

Remember how, at one time, you thought it was a good idea to teach your small child to ski? Remember how skiing seemed like a fun family activity: everyone outside in the brisk air—cheeks red, noses running—learning to overcome their natural (and perhaps evolutionarily adaptive) fear of insanely steep slopes? Remember?

If so, I have just one more question: What in the world were you thinking?

Perhaps, like me, you didn't understand that small children who ski grow up to be teenagers who ski. And trust me: you should never ski with your teenaged child.

Here are the top 10 reasons why:

1. **Teenagers' memories are short.** Your child will have no recollection of all those years when "skiing together" meant laboring hunchbacked down the slope, holding her skis between your skis, screaming "Pizza wedge! Make a pizza wedge with your skis!" (Only years later did we realize that our child had no concept of a "wedge" because our local pizza shop cut pizza into squares.)

2. **Teenagers don't want to ski with you.** They do not want to be seen on the same mountain as you. You ski like an old person. You have funny clothes. Your boots don't match your skis. You

stop too much. No offense, but they prefer to ride up the chair-lift with perfect strangers. But wait–first can they have $8.50 for a hot chocolate?

3. **Teenagers think that anything that costs a lot of money must be fun.** It's fun to outgrow your ski boots, jacket, and pants so that you need a new ensemble every winter. It's fun to ask for new deluxe racing skis for Christmas only to decide the following year that you want to try snowboarding. It's fun to take a ski vacation in Colorado, even though for the price of the lift tickets your family of four could:

    (a) Finance the next Ben Affleck movie;

    (b) Pay down the national debt;

    (c) Feed the country of Somalia.

    (The correct answer, of course, is "All of the above.")

4. **Unlike you, teenagers have no fear.** If you do somehow manage to ski with teenagers, they will lead you to the edge of a sheer 500-foot drop and leave you for dead. After 30 minutes of degrading whimpering, you will be forced to sidestep back up the mountain to find a safer trail. Unfortunately, this course of action leads to reason No. 5:

5. **Teenagers will never be seen with anyone who has side-stepped back up the mountain to find a safer trail.** They have their standards.

6. **Teenagers are mooches.** If your teenager expresses a willingness to ride up the chairlift with you, be afraid—be very afraid. By the end of the ride, she will have wrangled from you your good mittens, hand warmers, Chapstick, goggles (yours don't fog as much) and another $8.50 for hot chocolate.

7. **Teenagers won't listen when you talk about trees.** Unlike your teenager, you remember Sonny Bono. You know that trees

are not just pretty trail decorations supplied by Mother Nature, but rather lethal threats lying in wait for them. Yet no matter how carefully you explain to them the evil, insidious, dangers of trees, you still come off sounding like the paranoid lunatic they believe you to be.

8. **Teenagers claim you ski too slowly.** Sure, you stop frequently to rest, catch your breath, and confirm that your fingers–though you can no longer feel them–are still connected to your hands. However, this behavior will almost certainly annoy the teen, who, now in possession of your good mittens and hand warmers, is experiencing no such problem.

9. **Teenagers will destroy any shred of dignity you may still possess.** They will suggest that you ski down the hill first and they follow "in case you fall and need help getting up." They will steer you towards trails named after timid woodland creatures such as "Possum Hill" or "Chipmunk Run". On a recent ski trip, my 13-year-old pointed to a slope called "Lower Standard" and suggested, "That sounds like a good one for you, Mom!"

10. **Teenagers never hurt the day after.** The next day, as you try to raise yourself out of bed, reciting in order the muscle groups that are torturing you ("gluteus medius, gluteus maximus, gluteus minimus…"), your teen will be quietly swiping your ski mittens for another day on the slopes.

But here, finally, we have to acknowledge the major advantage of having teenagers: unlike small children, they can, in fact, ski on their own. While they do so, you can relax in a warm lodge, thawing your frostbitten body parts, blocking all memory of 500-foot drops, and savoring a hot chocolate for a mere $8.50.

Turns out that $8.50 is a reasonable price to pay to maintain the last shreds of your dignity.

Prom Night II: The Horror Continues

My problem, it seems, is that I don't speak "Prom."

It's a language I never expected to have much use for.

When I was a teenager, going to the prom was something you did once, so learning a new vocabulary for it would have been a waste of time.

My older daughter, however, is on her second prom, and I envision at least one more in her future before we are able to ship her off to the convent...I mean college. Consequently, she speaks fluent Prom. Since we don't speak it at home, I guess she just picked it up from the kids at school.

Now, the people at the dress stores, the limousine services, the beauty and tanning salons—they all speak Prom, too. Unfortunately, however, they still require a translator when speaking to my daughter.

This is because she does not yet speak "Visa."

I speak fluent Visa. As a result, I am suddenly very popular with the prom set.

Take the whole limousine issue. My daughter and her friends will pay for their limo rental—or so they tell me—but lack the credit card to reserve it.

This is where I come in. Apparently, I have been elected by the prom-goers as "The Parent Most Likely to be Railroaded into Doing Our Bidding." I am assigned the job of reserving a limousine.

Well now, limousines—*here's* a subject I know a great deal about. "Do they come in different colors?" I ask my daughter.

She frowns. Already she is rethinking the wisdom of my involvement.

"Just don't get anything too boxy," she advises.

I have no idea what a "boxy" limo looks like (made of cardboard? stackable?), so I decide simply to repeat this phrase to the limo rental people.

Happily, they understand "boxy." I'm treated to a lengthy explanation, during which the term "Euro" is introduced. Already I am in over my head. I ask if I can see the limo just to confirm that its construction involves no corrugated cardboard or duct tape.

Not only can I see the limo, but I'm invited to sit in it. I climb inside and make myself comfortable. The limo has seating for 10, a TV, a sound system, an ice bucket, and fancy glasses for (nonalcoholic) beverages. I am in heaven. After several minutes reclining with my eyes closed, the limo people gently suggest it's time for me to leave. I pull out my Visa card and tell them "I'll take it."

My language problems, however, don't stop with the limo rental. Another of my weak areas is fingernail decoration. Yet somehow I have agreed to help my daughter arrange for a manicure before prom.

I turn for help to my friend Lisa, who, by cutting my hair for years, has demonstrated an ability to work with the most desperate of materials. Lisa also manages never to laugh at me—at least, not to my face—for my ignorance of all the areas in which she excels: hair, nails, skin care, makeup.

However, when I ask Lisa about a manicure for my daughter, she suddenly begins speaking what may as well be Swahili, for all the sense I can make out of it.

"Does she have nails?" is the first thing Lisa wants to know.

I am convinced that this as a trick question. Who doesn't have nails? And yet Lisa does not seem to be joking and is waiting patiently for an answer.

Noting my confusion, Lisa tries again. "What I mean is, does she have a free edge?" I continue to stare blankly. I could swear that "free edge" is a term I learned in ski lessons.

"This is not my first language," I explain. "Do you speak any Tomboy?"

By this time, Lisa has assessed the situation. "I'm guessing that she wants a 'mani' and a 'pedi,'" she concludes.

Now I am not familiar with these words, but they sound to me like crimes for which people could serve hard time at the state penitentiary. I shrug and set up an appointment…for something.

"Just nothing too boxy," I tell Lisa, showing off my new command of Prom lingo.

She seems unsure how to respond. I think I have impressed her.

Since that first experience speaking a little Prom, I've been feeling more confident with the language—even helping my husband a bit. For example, when he looks at the Visa bill, he thinks that the limo people have charged us for *purchasing* the limo, rather than renting it.

I assure him that the rental amount must be in "euros."

What can I say? You just can't expect everyone to master languages the way I do.

The Dangers of Sleepover Camp—For Parents

Thinking about sending your child to sleepover camp? Think again. You may not be aware of the danger involved.

I'm not talking about tipping canoes or poison oak or tennis elbow or even the kind of post-lights-out education gleaned from smuggled copies of *Cosmo Girl*.

No, your hearty little camper will survive all that. The real risk is to you.

Why?

Because nothing reveals flaws in your parenting like sending your kid to camp.

I suspect this fact may come as a surprise to you—rather like the cost of camp itself—so allow me to elaborate.

Here are the top five reasons you should think twice about sending your child to sleepover camp, categorized by their potential for parental humiliation.

1. You have failed to provide for your child's most obvious fundamental needs.

Sure, your child owns an iPod, the latest Beyoncé CD, and stylish tank tops in 57 different colors. But inevitably, on the day she is leaving for camp, you will discover that she doesn't own a single pair of matching socks.

The cotton remnants that occupy space in her sock drawer seem to lack the key characteristics—heels, for example, and toes—that would identify them as footwear.

What, you wonder, had she been wearing to school? You recall a particularly brutal winter this year…Oh, well, too late to worry about that now.

2. You have failed to provide for your child's less obvious fundamental needs.

Inevitably, the sock issue forces you to confront the dreaded underwear question: Does she have enough? And what *is* enough, anyway?

Here is where our failures in the parenting department become most embarrassing.

A friend of mine asked her daughter, as she packed for camp, if she had enough underwear for the week. Her daughter cheerfully assured her that, yes, in fact, she had packed both pairs.

"What was she planning to do?" my friend wondered. "*Alternate* them?"

And as with socks, even when the quantity is sufficient, sometimes the quality leaves something to be desired. Another friend, recalling her mother's rule never to wear torn underwear lest she be hit by a car, bemoaned the tattered briefs in her son's duffel bag. "He doesn't even have anything to get hit by a car in!" she wailed.

3. You have failed to institute an appropriate summer bedtime.

You realize that the summer schedule at your house has become just a tad too relaxed when the camp director announces that "lights out" is at 9 p.m., and your little camper wonders, "What—before dinner?"

4. You have failed to establish appropriate "give-and-take" communication with the child.

Perhaps it's the rushed effect of camp pay phones, but most phone calls from camp tend to sound like this one, received last week by a fellow parent:

"Dad, OK, here's what we need: Pringles—the sour cream and onion kind; peach rings; two packs of Bubblicious gum…"

"Hey, how are you liking camp?"

"Dad, this is important. We need Skittles, and lots of them…"

5. You have failed to choose the correct camp.

After agreeing to your child's wish to attend a pricey basketball camp at a prestigious private school, where for five days campers learn about, practice, and play basketball nonstop from sunrise to sunset, you ask your child how she is liking camp.

"Too much basketball," she replies.

"It's a basketball camp! What was she expecting?" my husband wants to know. "More *fishing*?"

It hardly matters. For those parents who, like me, spent the first week of their child's sleepover camp skulking around the socks and underwear department at Target and overnighting her extra pairs (along with a camp-sized bag of Skittles), a bigger failure now weighs on our minds.

Somehow, in a week at home alone, we have failed to have any fun without them.

Lord of the Key Rings

It is the dregs of March and I am a prisoner in my own house.

My teenage daughter passed her driving test and I've come to the realization that I may never see her—or my car—again.

I'm not even going to get into which of them I will miss most. It wouldn't be fair. My car and I have been inseparable for years.

We went everywhere together: to soccer games, parent-teacher conferences, the grocery store, the beach. We got coffee together in the morning. My car brought me to dinner and the movies. It was always there, waiting for me, after a stressful doctor's visit or root canal. We took long drives, just the two of us.

Now, on occasion, I'll catch a glimpse of tail lights as the two of them—my daughter and my ride—cruise off down the driveway together.

I've taken to wandering about the house, fondling my car keys and muttering about the loss of "my precious."

I blame myself. After all, I brought the two of them together. I raised the child in my car. It was the only home she ever knew.

As an infant, my daughter was so content in her car seat that she would drift off to sleep—something that she never did elsewhere, like in her crib. So we spent hours in the car together—many of them sitting in our own driveway. She would snooze peacefully and I, the exhausted new mother, would enjoy the hypnotic effect of the windshield wipers going back and forth, back and forth. Often it wasn't even raining.

My daughter's first actual driving experience was at age 3. Having somehow jump-started my standard transmission while I chatted with her babysitter, she backed the car down the driveway and up onto my sitter's lawn. There, the car stalled—luckily, since at seven months pregnant I couldn't have waddled fast enough to catch it. Instead, I made a mental note to add her as a driver on our insurance policy.

At amusement parks, we would wait in line for an hour so my daughter could drive an antique car around a little track. Apparently, those cars are not supposed to leave the track. At least, that's what the teenaged attendant told us when the child ran over his foot, causing a six-car pileup. Afterwards, he had the nerve to suggest that my daughter was too young to drive.

"Actually," I informed him, "she's been driving longer than you have."

Through all the years that followed, as I drove her to birthday parties or music lessons or gymnastics or softball games, the car became our home on wheels. My daughter used this time to master the truly important aspects of driving: setting the radio stations, managing drinks in the cup-holder, adjusting the seat-warmers.

So now, on the rare occasions when she lets me ride with her, she lets me know who is in control.

She sets the music volume to nine, a level I'm pretty sure causes tinnitus in all mammals except, for some mysterious reason, humans between the ages of 12 and 18.

She blasts the heat until I've peeled off so much clothing that I actually need to add back layers to exercise at the gym.

She snitches all the change in my not-so-secret coin compartment to buy hazelnut iced coffees, and when I wonder where all the money went, she tells me "tolls."

Sometimes, though, if we stop at a store and she runs inside to do an errand, I'll turn on the windshield wipers, lean back in my seat, and watch them move back and forth, back and forth.

And I feel content that, for a while at least, I still have my precious.

Both of them.

Of iPods and Elbows and Things We Can't Control

In our household, things break on a daily basis. A computer goes on strike, our pool filter stops pumping, the toaster oven spontaneously bursts into flames. Our overworked clothes dryer heaves a big sigh, ceases all movement, and applies for workers' compensation benefits.

Most recently, the problem was my daughter's iPod. It decided to lose all 40 gazillion songs she had stored on it. They just up and vanished, without a trace.

However, these days, by age 14, kids are more resourceful than you expect or even want them to be. My daughter, for example, knew of the existence of special iPod doctors who can fix ailing iPods and retrieve lost songs. Moreover, she knew that these specialists reside *at the mall*. Even if they couldn't repair the iPod, well, the trip wouldn't be a total waste, would it?

So, we bundled up the sick iPod and carried it to the store, where we were directed to the technicians at the "Genius Bar." I liked this name, which suggested not only that the iPod doctors were very smart, but that they might serve me a vodka gimlet while I waited.

Sadly, no such luck. Instead, the technician plugged the iPod into some kind of life-support system and peered at a screen monitoring its vital signs. From his frown, I gathered that the prognosis wasn't good. After several minutes, he unplugged the lifeless iPod and laid it on the counter in front of me. I waited for him to offer an explanation, or at least last rites.

Instead, he shrugged. "Something happened to it," he said.

Now usually I appreciate specialists talking to me in language that I can understand. But this seemed to be taking it a bit far.

"That would be your...technical assessment?" I asked.

He handed me a new iPod. He was clearly tired of people asking why things happen.

But I was confused. If the best explanation that either the geniuses or the bartenders of the world can offer is "something happened," then whom *can* we look to for answers?

I needed to know, because more things were breaking.

That same week, my daughter—the one with the iPod—took a tumble in a soccer game. She does this quite a bit, actually, and I've learned not to be alarmed. Usually, she leaps back up, her face full of the righteous indignation she hopes will persuade the referee to blame her opponent. This time, however, she didn't get up.

The problem was her left elbow, and while over the next 24 hours everyone from EMTs and ambulance drivers to X-ray technicians and orthopedic surgeons offered a smorgasbord of diagnoses, the bottom line for my daughter was this: *something had happened* and her first high-school soccer season with all its hopes and dreams had vanished, like the songs in her iPod.

It made me reflect on how much in our lives can break down or even vanish without a trace because *something happened* that we don't understand.

Some of us get hung up in the hows and whys, while others, like my daughter, move on. As I was still holding the emergency room X-rays up to the sunlight in our kitchen to figure out where a medial collateral ligament attaches, she was already determining the fastest ride at the Topsfield Fair she could manage with her arm in a sling.

It didn't take me too many vodka gimlets to realize her way was best.

That's Right: We're Bad

My husband and I knew we were in trouble the minute we sat down at the school event.

The woman sitting next to us was holding a bouquet of pink roses for her child.

We looked around the room. Other parents were also holding flowers. We looked at each other.

"Darn," I said. (Well, okay, that wasn't exactly the word I used—I'm paraphrasing.)

"It happened again, didn't it?" my husband asked.

I nodded. My husband and I often feel like bad parents. We have an unfortunate tendency to show up at events for our children—performances, award ceremonies, inductions, graduations—empty-handed. While other children receive flowers or cards stuffed with cash, our daughters tend to get a smile and a hearty handshake. They have never been shy about pointing out this disparity.

Still, it persists. It's not that we're opposed to rewarding children for a job well done—we're just a little schedule-challenged. It's an accomplishment when we arrive at events early enough so we don't have to park in the fire lane.

Of course, as I surveyed the crowded room that evening, I could see that not *every* parent had brought flowers; however, almost everyone was busy focusing their cameras or checking the lighting for their camcorders.

"Did you bring the camera?" my husband asked.

"Did *you*?" I shot back. (OK, it wasn't particularly mature, but it was all I had.)

He sighed and thought for a moment. "Isn't there a camera on your cell phone?"

"Yes," I admitted. "And I've taken great photos of my pants leg, the carpet, and the inside of my purse, but never anything I was actually aiming at."

"Well, can you just hold it up and make it flash, so it *looks* like we're good parents?" He was joking. I think. Maybe not.

In any case, I knew it wouldn't work. To make it flash, I'd have to turn on the phone, and inevitably, in that exact nanosecond, it would start ringing, interrupting the ceremony, and adding a whole new dimension to our humiliation.

As if to make matters worse, the principal now announced that parents were not just welcome, but actually encouraged, to take photos. As each student's name was announced, the audience began to resemble a giant Whack-a-Mole game, with parents popping up to photograph their offspring and then disappearing back into their seats.

My husband and I tried to put a positive spin on things. We were not so much bad parents as simply "low-tech." He suggested that since we had no camera to take a photo, perhaps I could jump up and make a sketch of our daughter on my program.

He was joking again. I think.

I refocused on the flower idea.

"Maybe I could slip out before the end of the ceremony," I suggested. "Where can I get flowers really fast?"

"There are probably some nice ones growing in front of the school," he said.

I must have paused too long, because he added, "This time I really am joking."

He was right. I could just see the front-page photo in the next day's newspaper: a police flashlight shining in my face, I'd be clutching a fistful of tulips with bulbs still attached. The caption would read, "Mother of National Honor Society inductee caught pinching perennials during refreshments."

Somehow this didn't seem in keeping with the occasion.

In the end, I'm proud to say, our daughter got her usual smile and hearty handshake and seemed perfectly fine with it. I guess there's something to be said for keeping your children's expectations low. The best part was how impressed she was afterwards, as we walked to the car: "Wow," she said. "You didn't even park in the fire lane."

At least she recognizes when we've made an effort. Maybe we're not such bad parents after all.

PART 5

Life on the Sidelines: Kids' Sports

In Rugby, Protection Is Hardly the Name of the Game

I've spent years coddling and overprotecting my children. I don't like to brag, but I consider myself a master at it.

When my oldest daughter was an infant, I used to sneak into her room while she was asleep and hold a hand mirror to her mouth to be sure she was breathing.

While most mothers teach their children to look "right-left-right" when crossing the street, I made my kids look "right-left-right-left-right-left." Eventually, they realized that crossing the street just wasn't worth it.

I sliced the grapes in their school lunches until my older daughter told me to "cut it out."

"But they're a choke food!" I pleaded.

"Not when you're in high school!" she assured me.

I even bought fire escape ladders to put under each of my kids' bed. (Hint: It's best to remove these before your children become teenagers, because—trust me on this—they won't wait for a fire to escape.)

My coddling didn't stop as they grew older. Even when I became accustomed to the older child having a license, I would not let her drive her younger sister anywhere. When I finally gave in, I made the 12-year-old buckle herself into the middle of the backseat and shoved full backpacks and fluffy down parkas on either side of her. I was still searching for a ski helmet when they sped off together.

Of course, even I recognized that all good coddling had to end sometime.

So, this fall, when my older daughter left for college with all her limbs intact and a complete set of (expensively straightened) teeth, I counted myself an overprotective success story. My work was done.

At least, that's what I thought until my husband, younger daughter, and I attended our first Parent's Weekend at the older child's college. There, we were invited to watch her play her new favorite sport: rugby.

Here's how they define rugby in *The Nervous Mother's Dictionary:*

Rugby (rug' be): (1) A sport with all the hitting, tackling, and general violence of football, but with no helmets, padding, or protective gear beyond a mouth guard; (2) a sport in which an ambulance remains parked beside the playing field throughout the match; (3) an overprotective mother's worst nightmare.

I asked my daughter how she became involved in such an "interesting" sport.

"My friend Kendra used to play," she explained, "until she got the concussion."

"Too much information," I said, holding my hands over my ears.

"Our team has had three concussions," my daughter continued proudly. "But Kendra's was the worst."

By this point, my husband was eyeing the EMT's equipment, trying to see what they had in the way of oxygen.

The rules of rugby were hard to discern—especially with both hands over your eyes—but I learned that the game begins with what they call a "scrum." Here, a circle of players from both teams lock arms and butt heads while trying to "hook" the ball to their teammates using their feet. (This, thankfully, explained the rugby posters we had noticed around campus inviting fellow students to "support our hookers.")

As the two teams butted heads and pawed the ground with their feet, many of the women made the kind of noises I had heard before only in labor delivery rooms.

"Why are they making those noises?" my younger daughter wondered.

"Based on my experience," I replied, "I'd say they're ready to push."

I discovered that another key element in rugby is the rather oddly shaped ball. Apparently, a player cannot be tackled unless she is holding the ball. Therefore, whenever the ball was tossed or kicked near my daughter, I offered my best motherly advice: "Run away! Run away!"

Sadly, she did not run away. Instead, she caught the ball, ran a few yards down the field, and passed off to someone behind her.

"Did you see that?" I asked my husband excitedly.

"What?"

"As she ran down the field, she looked right-left-right-left-right-left."

He looked at me with pity. "You go ahead and cling to that if you need to."

I didn't need to; I had other resources. If my child went down, I had an EMT by my side and a hand mirror in my purse. I was ready for anything.

Every Parent's Nightmare: A Child's Relapse into Rugby

My daughter called home from college a few weeks ago and confessed that she had fallen back in with the wrong crowd. The girls she was hanging with were not only tough and prone to sudden acts of violence, a bunch of them were hookers. Before you get the wrong idea, let me clarify: my daughter was once again playing rugby—a sport in which players try to "hook" the ball.

It was hard for me to know how to respond. I believe I resorted to one of those high-pitched maternal "Mmmmms" that roughly translates as, "I know I don't have any say in this, but that isn't going to stop me from chewing off the inside of my mouth."

I had hoped that my older daughter had given up this violent sport, in which kneeing your opponent in the ribs is applauded by your teammates and rarely called by the referee. Last fall, my husband and I had been delighted to ship the child off to study in Denmark, a country where the national sport is making really nice pastries. We thought we had successfully refocused her attention.

But no, she admitted on the phone, once back on campus this spring she had lapsed into old habits. She was calling, in fact, to invite us to watch her play in a rugby tournament called "The Beast of the East."

Somehow, this wasn't what I had dreamed of for my daughter.

My husband and I decided to take her up on the tournament invitation for two reasons. First, we were flattered. Our daughter rarely wants to be in the same state as we are, never mind on the same athletic field. Second, rugby is a sport in which they actually keep the ambulance parked by the playing field, and my kids have always liked me to accompany them on ambulance rides. They feel it's best if I panic someplace where they can keep an eye on me.

As it turned out, our biggest parental trauma was not an ambulance ride, but rather the 5-minute shuttle-bus ride my husband and I took from the parking lot to the tournament playing field. In riding that bus, we learned that rugby breeds a different kind of parent.

As we took our seats, the man in front of us was already engaged in conversation with a couple across the aisle. "And last year, my daughter tore her ACL so badly she needed surgery and 6 months of rehab," he concluded with what sounded like pride.

"Yeah, in October our daughter had her second concussion," said the man across from him. "But it wasn't anywhere near as bad as the first one. She was only unconscious for 2 minutes."

His wife chimed in: "Her little sister is tougher. She's had two concussions and a broken nose." There was a murmur of admiration from the parents sitting within hearing distance.

"My daughter broke her septum," offered another mother.

"I didn't know you could break that!" said the first man in amazement.

"Yep, you can!" she bragged.

I leaned over and whispered to my husband, "Who ARE these people?"

"I don't know," he replied, "but if they want to be first to get off the bus, I say we let them."

After listening to the stories on that shuttle bus, watching the rugby match was a piece of cake. Our daughter managed to carry the ball a few times and pass it off to another player without ending up on the wrong side of a 20-person pig pile or—as far as we could tell—getting kneed in the ribs.

In fact, with so many rugby matches taking place on side-by-side playing fields, the spectators were in almost as much danger as the players. At one point, I was nearly flattened by a group of male players tackling an opponent so energetically that their enthusiasm extended beyond the line markers. Now, there was a time when I wouldn't have minded a group of college-aged men falling all over me, but that day has long since passed. (Sadly, in fact, it passed without this ever happening.)

By the end of the afternoon, my husband and I left the tournament relatively content. Our daughter's head seemed to be intact—or at least no different than it has always been—and I had suffered only minor self-inflicted bite wounds to my fingernails and the inside of my mouth.

However, we decided to forego the shuttle bus ride and walked the 3 miles to the parking lot. As we had learned from our daughter, you've got to be careful what crowd you hang with.

For This Group of Teen Girls, Sleepovers Are a Slam-dunk

My younger daughter recently asked us to host a sleepover party for her sixth-grade girls' basketball team.

"Why us?" I moaned, hoping to sound like the kind of tired, grumpy mom you wouldn't want anywhere near your friends.

She shrugged, but I knew why. I'm convinced the girls on the team got together and voted on which parents were the biggest suckers.

You think I'm kidding. However, I've noticed that while parents use the team roster to jot down other parents' names and cell phone numbers, the girls annotate their own rosters with vital facts like "owns a swimming pool," "has foosball table in family room," and "parents exercise zero control." I'm pretty sure we appear on the kids' rosters as "confirmed wussies."

So, living up to our press clippings, my husband and I agreed to have the party.

After all, how bad could it be? These were 11- and 12-year-old girls, right?

No, they are an 11- and 12-year-old basketball team. There's a difference.

These girls were not interested in painting their nails, braiding each other's hair or discussing the relative merits of Viggo Mortenson versus Orlando Bloom—a subject on which certain middle-aged moms wouldn't mind weighing in. (Do you think I watched those "Lord of the Rings" movies for the Orks?)

Oh, no. These girls came ready to play. Most arrived wearing their team warm-up shirts and pajama pants. I swear a couple even had red war paint under their eyes, but perhaps it was just high color.

My husband and I made the mistake of assuming that, because these particular girls are on the small side ("We call it 'vertically challenged,' Mom," chides my daughter), they would somehow be easier to control.

We forgot that this height deficiency is the linchpin of their basketball strategy—the key illusion they use to their advantage against the other teams.

Yes, these girls are small. Not quite hobbit-sized, but close. When they play other teams, our girls look directly into the opposing players' Adam's apple. We parents marvel at the size of these sixth-graders from rival towns—girls who seem to have ingested their Bovine Growth Hormone straight, rather than laced with milk.

But what our team lacks in height, they make up for in scrappiness. These are girls who "high-five" their teammates when they foul out in the first half of the game. These are girls who, after a collision—I swear, I've seen this—try to hide the blood dripping from their mouths so their coach won't pull them out of the game.

And so, during the course of that long sleepover evening, rather than help these young ladies crimp hair or file cuticles or make jewelry out of string, I became familiar with several important basketball terms.

For example, when the girls order so many pizzas that the stack of boxes effectively blocks a parent from entering the room, it's called *boxing out*. An alternate use of the term is when the five leftover pizza boxes ("We weren't really as hungry as we thought") consume so much space in the refrigerator that not even a baby carrot can be wedged in.

Driving (or diving) into the paint is a game in which nine girls lift and hurl the 10th into a pile of sleeping bags fortified with a beanbag chair. If they miss, and Projectile Girl hits the wall, she is "in the paint." She can remain there for no more than three seconds, regardless of whether both eyes have completely refocused.

Fouling out, also known as *fowling out*, happens when the shrieks of adolescent girls become so loud and high-pitched they panic the chickens at a neighboring farm, reducing egg production the next day.

Double dribble occurs when little rivulets of both orange soda and root beer dribble off the counter and then pool, colorfully, in the silverware drawer.

When one smuggled basketball and two lamps hit the floor at the same time, frightening the pet rabbit so she leaps into her water dish, it's called a *slam-dunk*.

A *rebound* occurs just when you think that the girls are so exhausted that they will sleep until the following Wednesday. Instead, at daybreak they next morning, 10 pairs of eyes simultaneously snap open and voices resume their pre-sleep decibel level. It's as if no sleep occurred at all. (Which, in some quarters of the house, it didn't.)

Our evening with the basketball team reminded my husband and me that we no longer compete in the same league as these girls. Although we clearly can drive and charge and probably even dribble a bit (at least in our sleep), we just don't rebound like we used to.

That's all right. If next to our daughter's name on the team roster the girls scrawl "not worth it—parents ugly when deprived of sleep," we're happy to pass along hosting privileges to another set of parents. We'll let the second-string wussies give it a shot.

Don't Talk Track to Me, Young Lady!

For years as my daughters grew up, I was a soccer parent. It was a role I was comfortable with. I knew what to do and what not to do.

- I knew that when an opposing player took down my child, I should scream "Yellow card!" but when my daughter took out that same opponent, I should yell, "She was just playing the ball!"
- I knew not to shout "You're off-sides!" to my daughter within hearing of the referee.
- I knew where to find a Dunkin Donuts near every soccer field in the county, but not to feed donut holes to "Under-10" players after the match unless you want to do a lot of unpleasant cleanup of the car upholstery.

Things became more complicated, though, when the years passed and my younger daughter took up track in high school. I had so much to learn.

First of all, track requires an entirely new vocabulary. It turns out that words like "splits" and "heat" and "seed" don't mean at all what you think they do.

Also, the sport revolves around numbers—times, heights, distances—which can be challenging to a math-phobic person like me. In soccer, the only numbers I had to understand were "Visitors 6, Home

0;" however, in track, people often speak entirely in numbers, without inserting so much as a unit of measure for context. For example, my daughter will say things like, "Today I ran a 400 in 61.7 and a 200 in 27.8, but next time I might do the 800 because I want to beat 2:26."

"Great!" I respond, smiling brightly.

"You have no idea what I'm talking about, do you?" she'll ask.

"No!" I smile even more brightly. "Not a clue!"

The other thing I've learned about track meets is that you can often drive for 45 minutes to get to a competition in which your child participates for only 27.8 seconds. It seems like a lot of work for under 30 seconds of excitement. Reminds me of some of my early dating experiences.

My biggest issue with track has been with the javelin, an event that my daughter took up last year. During the previous season I had been okay—mostly—watching her jump backwards over a bar to land on her neck (which pretty much sums up the high jump as far as I'm concerned). However, hurling sharp spears into the air was another matter. Even worse: my daughter was not the only one throwing them. During warm-ups, athletes from both teams were lobbing spears in every direction. In my opinion, all these javelin throwers should be kept much farther apart—for example, in different counties.

So, during track meets I tend to place myself some distance from the javelin event—someplace I can hyperventilate in private. Once there, I alternately cover and uncover my eyes, muttering whispered warnings like, "Watch out!....Look behind you!....Incoming!....Stay low!"

However, I thought my worst nightmare had been realized when my daughter informed me that she was participating in a "javelin relay."

"A javelin relay?" I repeated.

She nodded.

I looked at her a long time without speaking. "You mean," I finally asked, "you have to catch it?"

Sometimes my children find me very amusing.

She explained that in a javelin relay everyone throws their javelin from the same place and they just add together the team's best distances.

I breathed a sigh of relief. If all a javelin relay involves is math, then the only person likely to get skewered is me.

I Am Strong, I Am Electable, I Am Soccer Mom

I never imagined I had a chance at being president of the United States, but with Sarah Palin's 2008 run for vice president, I started to rethink that belief. I sensed that certain doors had opened up for me.

Now granted, I don't have any experience in government, but that's not the point. Sarah Palin was a hockey mom, and I am a soccer mom; finally, in our great country, that is starting to count for something.

Oh, I know skeptics abound, but being a soccer mom teaches you a lot about politics. For 17 years while I sat on bleachers, scraped mud off of cleats, and drove station wagons full of kids with smelly socks through the Dunkin Donuts drive-thru, I have been developing an impressive resume of political skills. Here are just a few:

I know what it's like to be in the hot seat. Believe me, no one has sat for more hours on a folding chair with the sun in her eyes and sweat dripping down her back than I have. But do you know what? I've also had worse. Being in the hot seat is nothing compared to sitting on metal bleachers when it's 31 degrees outside and the only thing between you and that icy-cold metal is a thin layer of worn denim. That, my friend, is where a soccer mom learns to be tough.

I know how to be nonpartisan. As a soccer mom, you must applaud during the introduction of the other team even though you know that they pull shirts, grab arms, and elbow your players in the ribs. Your child's team would never play dirty like that. Occasionally, it may *seem* as if your team is getting overly aggressive, but they are only being "spirited."

I know how to play by the rules (when they suit me). Soccer moms know that we must not dispute the rules with the referees, regardless of how blind the refs are to blatant handballs, illegal slide tackles, and the subtleties of the off-sides rule. Instead, when our team receives a bad call, we provide shock and "Awwwww!"

Soccer moms, by the way, gladly accept make-up calls.

I can mobilize the masses. Even after all these years, I can still organize a bleacher full of parents to do "the wave." However, I have learned through hard experience never to do it with a half-full cup of hot chocolate.

I know how to create jobs. During the many years my husband coached youth soccer and I was his underappreciated lackey (or, as my resume now states, Vice Coach), I appointed people to be snack coordinators, phone callers, ball girls, and raffle-ticker sellers. Believe me, I can create jobs like nobody's business.

I know how to feed the hungry. I have fed hungry hordes of U12 players countless orange sections, grapes, and chocolate-chip cookies. I learned from personal experience how much hordes can eat.

I know how to respond in times of emergency. No matter what the crisis, it's important to appear calm and in control. A true soccer mom never rushes onto the field unless her child is unconscious, and even then, she doesn't walk fast. Instead, she calmly pushes her phone's speed dial number for the local ambulance and says, "Yep, it's us again...."

I know the ins and outs of fundraising. Soccer moms sell mums. We eat at more pizza fundraisers than anyone with a middle-aged metabolism should. We even barter with friends who are raising money for their kid's class trip or girl scout troop ("I'll take a wreath if you buy a chocolate bar.") Consequently, we own more Christmas gift-wrap than Santa.

I know how to protect our children. I am pro-mouth guard. A good soccer mom tells her child horror stories about young girls who spend the rest of their life saddled with bad teeth.

I understand the tactics of ground warfare. I can spot an off-sides trap a bleacher away. I know the value of a strong defense. But I don't believe in the draft. I'm a firm believer in tryouts.

So, there you have it: my qualifications to run for president on a soccer-mom platform. I think it compares well to a hockey-mom platform, don't you?

And if I don't make it to the White House, perhaps I can at least get one of my daughters a shot on "Dancing with the Stars."

PART 6

Pets and Parasites

And They Called It...Bunny Love

My family claims that I have lost my marbles over a bunny.

I maintain that there is nothing unnatural in my actions toward, or feelings about, this rabbit.

To begin with, it's not even my bunny. The bunny belongs to my 10-year-old daughter. Just because the bunny lives in my office, sleeps at my feet, shares my vegetables, and answers to the name I gave her doesn't mean it's my bunny.

Bun-Bun is not mine simply because I litter-trained her, feed her, pat her incessantly, scratch behind her ears, and talk to her as if she were my therapist. I am merely caring for this bunny while my daughter is at school—also, while she is playing sports, or at piano lessons, or sleeping at a friend's house. Really, it is largely her bunny.

And—be honest now—if you had an adorable cinnamon-colored bunny with long droopy ears and big eyes and a little wiggly black nose, wouldn't you bring it with you to book group?

So, you see, the problem is not me, but my family. Or, at least that part of my family that didn't want a bunny in the first place and stomped his feet and said, "No more pets!" and made all manner of bad faces. That would be the husband part of the family.

Also problematic is that part of the family that shrieked like a ban-shee when she discovered that Bun-Bun had sneaked into her room and chewed clean through her computer cord. This would be the older daughter part of the family.

(Personally, I don't think it is fair to blame Bun-Bun for the computer cord when we didn't actually see her do it. My daughter has many friends that go in and out of her room, and I've noticed that some of them have very sharp teeth.)

My husband was dealing well with my rabbit relationship, up to a point. That point was the evening when we were supposed to celebrate our 20th anniversary with dinner out, but Bun-Bun had eaten a pencil eraser, and I was concerned she was sick. After waiting patiently for an hour while I monitored everything that went into and came out of Bun-Bun, my husband wondered aloud whose needs were more important, his or the rabbit's?

In retrospect, I realize that I should have responded more quickly, but I was thinking.

My teenager claims that, in truth, she does not dislike the bunny, "But I think I'd like it better if you liked it less," she adds. (Interestingly, this explains why my daughter never got along with her younger sister. If only we hadn't *liked* the new child!)

Still, on occasion, she moans: "You prefer that bunny to your children!"

I explain to her that—at least on the majority of days—this is not true. I do have to admit, however, that living with a bunny has certain advantages over living with adolescent and teenage children. For example:

- Bun-Bun does not say "yuck" when I tell her what's for dinner. (In fact, not only does she eat all her vegetables, but she stands on her hind legs and begs for them.)

- Bun-Bun does not ask for another new winter coat because they are on sale. (She's perfectly content with the current model.)

- Bun-Bun doesn't talk on the phone for hours. (Indeed, Bun-Bun doesn't talk—sometimes an advantage in its own right.)
- Bun-Bun doesn't tell me that my clothes are "fine for someone of your era." (She finds my clothes tasteful…or, occasionally, tasty.)
- Given sufficient food and drink, Bun-Bun can be left alone in the house for brief stretches of time. (Given sufficient food and drink, a teenager left alone will throw a party for her 30 closest friends.)

By the same token, bunnies have certain intrinsic advantages over husbands. I'm thinking, for instance, that:

- Bun-Bun doesn't leave the newspaper strewn all over the counter. (She keeps it neatly in her litter box.)
- Bun-Bun doesn't turn down the heat in the house to the "frozen tundra" setting. (She happily snuggles next to the space heater with me.)
- Bun-Bun doesn't open the mail and leave all the ripped envelopes for me to throw away. (If she were to open the mail, she would eat the envelopes.)
- Bun-Bun won't ask me to help paint the deck this spring.

Given all this, is it any wonder that I'm so taken with this small, soft, furry creature, who hops around my house, chews my slipper when she wants to be patted, and licks my face when I give her a slice of banana? Am I really going overboard in my affection for her?

I hardly think so.

Naturally, Bun-Bun has certain limitations, and I recognize this.

She wasn't, for example, able to add a lot to the book group meeting, but I really can't fault her for that.

After all, I hadn't finished reading her the book.

Of Mites and Men: How They Can Ruin Your Sleep

It's my firm belief that things are microscopic for a reason, and that reason is so we don't have to look at them. If we're really lucky, we don't even have to know they exist.

But there are people who don't understand these simple rules for happy, oblivious living. One such person is my allergist.

Here we have a man who has devoted his entire professional career to educating people about invisible things, like dust mites. Dust mites, for those of you who were—like me—happily oblivious, are microscopic relatives of spiders that live in everyone's mattresses, comforters, and pillows. They feast (are you ready for this?) on our dead skin flakes.

I know, I know! Believe me, I never wanted to know that much about what was going on in anyone's bedroom, *including* my own.

To be honest, I'm not sure what I had been expecting when I scheduled an appointment to be tested for allergies. All I knew was that, about a year ago, someone had turned on a faucet in the back of my throat and left it running. At night, I rattled in my sleep like a 95-year-old man hocking a loogie.

So, I kept my appointment for the tests despite the fact that the woman on the phone used scary words like "skin pricks" and "needles" and "your insurance won't cover this."

As it turned out, the needle-sticking went okay—except for the part where I got all clammy and dizzy and almost passed out. The nurses tried to tell me that this happened because I hadn't eaten lunch. I explained that, no, this happened because they were sticking needles into me. It's amazing how people can ignore the obvious.

Far worse, though, was the emotional distress the doctor provoked by informing me I am allergic to things that are invisible. What was he thinking? Had he failed to notice the word "hypochondriac" on my ID bracelet?

He then proceeded to show me photos of dust mites, which don't look invisible at all when they are enlarged about a million times, but rather quite gross and frightening. I'm certain I saw some of these same hairy, eight-legged, pincer-faced creatures in "Jurassic Park." In fact, I'm now firmly convinced that it was a dust mite that got Samuel L. Jackson.

Sadly, this doctor offered no end of helpful information—all without my express written consent. I mean, did I really need to hear that your average mattress is home to somewhere between two million and 10 million dust mites? I'm convinced that I could have lived my entire life happily without knowing this.

Unruffled by the fact that I now had my fingers in my ears and was humming the national anthem, the doctor continued. He explained that it is not actually the mites themselves to which people are allergic; rather, it is the "droppings" that these creatures leave on your bedding after they have dined on the human skin flakes.

I couldn't help but ask him, "Does your wife appreciate you bringing this level of specificity into the bedroom?" He didn't respond, but he did jab me with a couple more needles, which I took as a kind of a response.

Since that unhappy appointment, I've learned there's a solution to sharing your bed with dust mites. By encapsulating everything (your mattress, box spring, comforter, pillows, and—perhaps, though I'm not sure about this—your partner) in a special protective coating, you can separate yourself from any eight-legged residents of your bedroom.

Of course, sleeping on the special vinyl covering also makes you feel like a bed-wetter. However, I feel that this is a small price to pay to for protection from these microscopic Velociraptors.

If only I had been able to warn Samuel L. Jackson.

Go Fish! Or Why I'm *So* Done with Pets

It's 1:39 a.m., and I'm staring at a fish.

I normally don't show much interest in tropical fish at this hour in the morning, or—truth be told—ever. In fact, I don't really like fish, except perhaps those that appear on my plate broiled and served with a creamy tarragon sauce.

The fish isn't mine; it belongs to my older daughter, and during the move from her college dorm room to her first apartment, she asked me to babysit. Perhaps this is an audition of sorts for the day—a long time in the future, I hope—when she might ask me to babysit for her children. If so, I'm in big trouble.

I have forgotten to feed the fish for 2 days.

That explains why I suddenly sat bolt upright at 1:38 a.m. and why I'm watching this fish so closely. I'm trying to figure out if I have damaged it—in particular, if it is swimming upside down.

It's harder to determine than you might think. The fish has a medium-sized fin on top (well, it's on top now) and both a large and a small fin underneath. I could be mistaken, but it seems to me that it used to be the other way around.

I'm trying not to worry. I'm not even sure that swimming upside down is a bad thing for fish. Now, *floating* upside down is bad—of this I'm certain. But swimming upside down might simply be a way to pass the time when you live in a flower vase.

I recall from my childhood TV-viewing that Flipper would sometimes swim upside down. Of course, Flipper was a dolphin, not a fish, but at 1:40 a.m., I feel this kind of distinction is splitting hairs.

Still, I stay put, watching for other signs of permanent damage.

Oh, I had warned my daughter, all right. When she told me she was leaving the fish with me, I replied with a quick and resounding, "No!"

She responded as she had to every other "no" in her life. She ignored it.

I assured her that I couldn't be trusted with living things. The fact that she had survived for 22 years under my care was a fluke. It could never be repeated.

She laughed. She thought I was joking.

Finally, I played the claustrophobia card. I can't stand to see living creatures confined to cages, tanks, or—in this case—a flower vase.

She tried the "their brains are so small, it doesn't matter" argument.

"It matters to me," I explained. "I empathize with small-brained creatures."

My daughter paused. I'm sure there are a lot of smart comebacks to this, but this was a girl in desperate need of a favor. "It's only a week…" she wheedled.

In the end, I caved. It was only a week; what could possibly go wrong?

My daughter handed me the feeding instructions and informed me that the fish's name was Princess (though, she quickly explained, the fish doesn't answer to it).

"Good to know," I said. "I'll take good care of her."

"Him," my daughter corrected. "Princess is a male."

I nodded. How silly of me not to have known.

Now, days later, as I play this conversation back in my mind, I suddenly feel ready to return to bed.

I realize that with a name like Princess, swimming upside down may be the least of this little guy's problems.

Don't Let the Bed Bugs Bite

The hotel room looks like it was just hit by a tsunami. Sheets and blankets are torn off the bed, the comforter has been tossed in a corner, and the bare mattress is completely overturned and leaning upright against the wall. A framed painting that had been hanging above the bed is lying face down on the desk.

In the middle of the bathtub, there is a suitcase.

No, this is not the aftermath of a Charlie Sheen party. This is the work of bed bugs.

Well, okay, the bed bugs didn't actually *make* this mess. In truth, I did. But bed bugs—or at least my paranoid and obsessive inspection for them—was what caused it.

Now granted, I'm paranoid about and obsessed by a lot of things— or so my husband will tell you. But New York City is currently experiencing a bed-bug plague of almost Biblical proportions, and I travel there a lot. I want to make sure that what bites in the Big Apple stays in the Big Apple.

Every time I come home from a business trip in New York, I show my husband what I'm convinced are bed-bug bites:

"Look," I insist. "Look at this on my arm."

"That's your elbow," he replies. "You've always had that."

"No, above that. Look at those red spots."

He pokes at it. "How did you get spaghetti sauce above your elbow?"

Actually, as it turns out, it was pizza sauce (hey, it's hard to eat on a moving train), but I still refuse to take any chances. That's why I've read all the literature. I've learned how to avoid bringing home any bed bugs I encounter on the road.

For example, while staying at a hotel, the minute you take off the clothes you're wearing, you are supposed to seal them in a plastic bag. The last time I stayed in New York, I put them in a trash bag and—not that I was being obsessive, mind you—tied it into 12 different knots, including a butterfly knot and a double-overhand. Then—because I had forgotten to squeeze out all the air—I couldn't squish the bag into my suitcase; it kept ballooning out in every direction. I finally had to take out all 12 knots, release the air, and try it again. It took 3 tries to get it right and 2 glasses of wine on the train afterwards to put it all behind me.

Another rule is: don't bring into your house the clothes you've been wearing on the road. As a result, once I arrive home from the train station, I call my husband from the garage. He brings a bathrobe down to the basement where I take off all my clothes. (It sounds like this has the potential for fun, but in reality, not so much.) The clothes go into the washing machine and I immediately take a shower, feeling like Karen Silkwood.

Still, in case all these precautions don't work, I've bed-bug proofed our bedroom.

Based on expert advice, I've wrapped double-sided tape around the bed's casters and stuck it around the bottom of the box spring. No bed bugs are going to scurry across those barriers! Of course, all this sticky stuff around our bed makes it a little tough for the humans, too ("Nancy, I'm sticking to the mattress again!"), but, hey, it's a small price to pay.

Lately, with the bed-bug infestation spreading nationwide, I no longer restrict my inspection routine to New York hotels. During Parents' Weekend at our daughter's college in Vermont, my husband and I arrived at our hotel at 10 pm; you can imagine his dismay as I began crawling around on the floor with a flashlight, peering into dark corners and behind nightstands, headboards, and pictures hanging above the bed.

He also wasn't real keen about ripping all the sheets and blankets off the bed and helping me lift the mattress and box spring so we could inspect both sides. (Certainly, these weren't the kind of late-night shenanigans he had envisioned in the olden days when we booked a night in a hotel.) By the time my inspection was done, we were exhausted and surrounded by a level of devastation not seen since Hurricane Sandy.

To date, I haven't actually found a bed bug in all my searching. However, I do have more sympathy for celebrities like Charlie Sheen who trash hotel rooms. Perhaps he's not looking for trouble—just bugs.

PART 7

The College Years—Theirs, Not Yours

Forcing, er, Helping Your Teen to Choose a College

I believe that God created the teenage years to help ease the pain of launching our children into the world.

During the teen years, though we parents cherish our offspring as much as always, we start to envision a time when we once again will have enough hot water for a shower; when we can watch our own TV shows or use the computer for five minutes; when we will no longer be derided as "the least cool people on earth."

So, even before most teenagers have considered moving away to college, we parents have begun to consider it for them.

Having been through this process recently, I can offer some advice to parents who need to "move their child along" on the path to choosing a college. Before you start scheduling interviews for them or tacking glossy brochures on the refrigerator, you'll need to answer four key questions:

1. How much are you willing to pay?

Let's face it, college tuition is steep, and when considering this cost, it's important to avoid a knee-jerk reaction like, "That's more money than I earn in a year!" Thinking in purely economic terms like that will get you nowhere.

Instead, as with any kind of extortion, you must carefully consider the alternatives. In this case, the alternative is having the child continue to live with you. Trust me: when viewed in this way, college tuition is a value.

2. How far away should you send your child?

Given that there are no accredited universities in Antarctica, really, no place is too far.

Remember, you have just forked over quite a large sum to get the teenager out of the house. You don't want him to be like one of those pets who, when transported to a different part of the country, is able to find his way home weeks later, looking starved and dirty (and, in the case of your student, carrying an enormous duffle bag of laundry). No, you want him someplace where he will stay put, someplace off the beaten path, someplace like…Greenland.

3. How can you get your teenager to settle on a school?

At first, your child will appear to have no interest in selecting a college. For teens, choosing a place where they can take courses that are even harder than those in high school is like having them decide in which arm they would like the tetanus booster. Why would they care?

Eventually, though, they will find things about college that interest them. Key among these things is: getting away from you.

However, other factors do come into play—for instance:

- whether the college is close to a beach or good skiing
- whether the dorms are co-ed by floor or by room
- whether the campus has enough open space to play Ultimate Frisbee
- whether any students on their campus tour were "hot."

And speaking of the campus tour, here's a word of warning: most teenagers decide on a college based almost entirely on how much they like the tour guide. If the tour guide appears cool, has multiple piercings, and can walk backwards without tripping on the sidewalk, the college is rated highly. If, on the other hand, your tour guide wears polyester pants, it won't matter how new the science center is, you can kiss that college goodbye.

The Tour Guide Principle can be problematic because most of the students who volunteer to lead tours are—let's face it—geeks. I know; I used to lead campus tours. So, if you really want your child to look favorably on a particular school, it's important to check out the tour guides in advance, rejecting any who sport pocket protectors or t-shirts that say "Nietzsche Rocks!" Instead, see if the school has any tour guides who drive hot cars, surf, or cut classes on a regular basis. These are the students your teen will admire and want to emulate.

4. How well will both you and your teen deal with the separation?

It's true: when the time draws near for your teenager to leave for school, both of you actually may begin to believe that you will miss each other. Don't be fooled by this. It is like the honeymoon period of a marriage—the reason it seems so good is because it has no connection to reality. Hold firm. Act like a parent; that is, say something so completely stupid that it will remind your child why she needs to leave immediately. (Note: almost any sentence you utter will do.)

And don't worry: not only will both of you survive this separation, you'll be amazed by how much smarter and cooler you'll seem to the child by Parent's Weekend, when she desperately wants to be taken out for dinner.

Luckily, I understand that there are many fine restaurants in Greenland.

Guess Who Came to Dinner?
We Weren't Sure…

Over the Thanksgiving holiday, my older daughter came home from college for the first time.

At least, I thought it was my daughter. She did, in fact, resemble the child that had left home ten weeks earlier and she wore a sweatshirt with the name of her college printed in 5-inch block letters. Plus, she knew the combination to get into our garage, although this is not a true test, as my children share this information freely with classmates, delivery people, and random strangers—in other words, anyone who asks.

But apart from these things, the intruder bore little resemblance to my daughter.

First of all, as she entered the house, she announced at full volume: "You don't know how wonderful it is to be home!"

Now, I believe I've heard these words somewhere before—I think Dorothy utters some variation on them in "The Wizard of Oz"—but I know for a fact that they have never been spoken by anyone to whom I've given birth.

Next, she rummaged through the kitchen cupboards, which for years have held nothing she deemed even remotely edible and exclaimed, "Look at all this great food!"

Then, she emptied the clean dishes out of the dishwasher and loaded a few of her cups and water bottles from school. Finally, she moved upstairs and, in the space of several hours, proceeded to do four loads of laundry.

It was in the laundry room that I finally confronted her, brandishing a fireplace poker.

"Who *are* you?" I accused. "And what have you done with my daughter?"

She gave a little laugh and flitted off to iron a shirt. Clearly, she was dodging the question. In politics, they call this a "non-denial denial." I wasn't fooled.

Over the next four days, my husband and I observed the Stepford child closely—always from a safe distance, so as not to provoke her. We noticed further clues that the intruder was not our daughter. For example:

- She spoke to her sister. In full sentences.
- These sentences did not include threats.
- She actually told a friend that she could not go shopping because she had to do *school work*.
- She listened to something her father said without her head spinning around.
- She sat in the living room on a Friday night and wrote a paper on Kreb's cycle. What's more—though I know this really pushes the envelope in terms of believability—the paper wasn't due till the following week.

However, just as I was about to confront the intruder again, I saw signs that my older daughter was still in there somewhere, lurking beneath this new college-student exterior.

For example, on Sunday afternoon, I found her rummaging through her sister's dresser. She was cataloging—with high moral outrage—the items that had been stolen from her room ("She took this sweatshirt?!"), while simultaneously evaluating what she, in turn, might lift.

The college student held up one of her sister's newest shirts. "Does she wear this?"

"Well," I hedged, "I'm sure she'll let you borrow it."

"No, I mean, will she *miss* it?"

Now this intruder was beginning to sound familiar.

In fairness, my older daughter did then pose these same questions to her sister, who replied that yes, she could wear the shirt, but no, she could not take it back to college with her.

When the 18-year-old had left the room, I turned to my middle-schooler. "You'll never see that shirt again," I predicted.

"I know," she sighed.

The mysterious intruder may have hoodwinked her parents for a while, but it was going to take a better disguise before she could pull one over on her little sister.

The Hardships of College Life: Am I Missing Something?

Last year, my husband and I sent our oldest child off to college and experienced the typical assortment of parental worries. Would she eat right? Who would take care of her if she became ill? And, most importantly, why were all the dorm rooms surrounding hers filled not with bubbly co-eds but with large, sweaty football players?

That was last year. Now in the midst of her sophomore year, our daughter has settled nicely into college life, and we have calmed down. In fact, what used to be worry has transformed into something entirely different—a feeling I have trouble putting a name to.

Could it be… envy?

Consider this recent round of emails:

Mom,

The food here is not as advertised. Last night, there were only 3 choices for dinner: chicken marsala with linguini, stir-fried pork with snow peas, or couscous salad with peppers and olives. There's never any variety. Maybe you can send me $30 a week so I can buy some groceries.

Your Loving Daughter

Darling Daughter,

Last night we had only three choices for dinner here, as well. However, it turned out we had only enough peanut butter for one sandwich, so that left two options: the box of Sponge Bob macaroni and cheese or the box of Scooby Doo. We went with Scooby. Nobody complained for fear of spending the rest of the evening blowing orange powdered cheese out of both nostrils.

Mom

P.S. If I had $30 a week to send you, I'd pay someone to do my grocery shopping.

Hi, Mom,

I'm just back from a weekend in Montreal where we ate at some great French restaurants and danced at some cool clubs. I'm applying to study abroad next fall in Denmark—is that in Europe?—and also may take a winter term course in Costa Rica, studying the flora and fauna. Not sure what fauna is, but I'm hoping for a nice pre-season tan.

Hasta la vista!

Your Eldest

Hola, Eldest!

I'm just back from an exciting trip to the dentist where I learned I need a root canal. This weekend I'm planning to go to the dry cleaners and, if I'm lucky, bring some soda cans to recycling. We may have to travel all the way to Hartford for your sister's spring soccer tournament. Do you think I can get a pre-season tan in Hartford?

Mom

P.S. Let us know if we can bring you back some insurance.

Dear Mom,

No insurance, thanks, but a red convertible is always welcome.

I'm off to a philosophy lecture on Kant and Aristotle. After that, I have to create a plan to save an inner-city school for my urban sociology class. By the way, I think some of the presidential candidates may be visiting campus this spring—they're all courting the student vote.

Your Darling Daughter

Dear Darling,

Not too many lectures around here this week. I did have a little chat with the bunny concerning the difference between her litter box and her food dish, and how she might try to keep them separate in her mind and daily habits. Plus, Dad and I had a long philosophical debate about whether it's best to put clothes in the washing machine before or after filling it with water, but I don't think his heart was really in it because he kept trying to wedge the ironing board between us and back out of the room.

The only person stopping by to ask our support is that little Girl Scout pushing cookies. Do you think it's possible to go into hyperglycemic shock from too many Thin Mints?

Your Loving Mother

Yes, as you can see from these emails, our worries concerning our daughter's college experience were unfounded. Her student life seems pretty good, especially in comparison to the real life that this college education is supposed to prepare her for—that is, the real life of talking to your rabbit, eating Scooby Doo macaroni and cheese, and traveling to Hartford for summer fun. She will hardly believe the things she has to look forward to!

I think I won't worry her about it just yet.

PART 8

Holidays and Other Perils of the Season

Good Gravy! Diary of a Thanksgiving Hostess

With the holidays approaching and everyone preparing to host family and friends, I thought I might share the details of my most recent Thanksgiving hosting experience. I like to think, as the saying goes, that if you can't be a good example, you can at least be a horrible warning.

Wednesday—The Day Before

9 a.m. Have a full 27 hours before guests arrive. Plan to make three appetizers, two kinds of stuffing, and three pies. In spare time, will create festive decorations out of common household items.

10 a.m. Plan to impress guests with unique pumpkin chiffon pie, involving 12 ingredients (8 more than usual limit)! Also intend to make wild rice and mushroom stuffing, but must convince children that sliced mushrooms are something else…perhaps really tiny slices of bread?

11 a.m. Recipe for wild rice and mushroom stuffing involves something called Dutch oven. Have carefully examined oven, and it appears to be American. Drat.

11:15 a.m. Decide to skip pretentious stuffing requiring appliances from the Netherlands. Instead, choose recipe that relies heavily on words, "Pepperidge Farm."

12 p.m. With aisles at grocery store overflowing with pumpkin and cranberry sauce, why am I the only shopper searching for flaked coconut?

12:10 p.m. Pie recipe calls for 16-ounce can of pumpkin. Store carries only 15-ounce cans. Do I make only 15/16ths of pie? Inquire if store manager has number for pumpkin-pie hotline.

1 p.m. Ask teenage daughter to create pie crusts. Currently, daughter is on couch with boyfriend, watching DVD. Does not appear to be in crust-making mood.

2 p.m. Am staring at partially consumed bag of pecans. Exactly how many pecans constitute 3 ounces? Am certain that there is a mathematical formula involved here. Must find a child.

2:20 p.m. Younger daughter refuses to be engaged by pecan word problem. Asks to be driven to the movies.

3 p.m. In effort to calculate 3 ounces of pecans, weigh self on bathroom scale with and without bag of pecans. Bizarrely, weigh 1/2 pound less while holding bag. Can only conclude that pecans somehow cause weight loss!

4:30 p.m. Teenager announces she is going to work. What about my pie crust? "It's only Wednesday!" she replies.

6 p.m. Still puzzling over "It's only Wednesday" remark. Call husband on cell phone to purchase pre-made crusts.

7 p.m. Pumpkin chiffon pie recipe requires something called jelly roll pan. What in God's name is jelly roll? And who invents names for pans?

8 p.m. Notice that label on pumpkin can contains recipe for simple pumpkin pie with few ingredients and fewer steps. Huzzah! Will make this pie instead.

8:05 p.m. Disaster! Pumpkin pie recipe requires one can evaporated milk. Wonder: If leave regular milk on counter for several hours, does it become evaporated milk?

8:10 p.m. Send husband to store for evaporated milk.

10 p.m. Discard magazine with feature article on "How to Dress Up Your Thanksgiving Table." Was never all that good at dressing up children, and they had legs that moved.

11 p.m. Apple and pecan pies done. However, pumpkin pie has baked for 65 minutes, and knife inserted into center still does not come out "clean," but rather covered in soupy, pumpkin stuff.

11:05 p.m. At 70 minutes, decide that "clean knife"—much like "clean child"—is relative term. Knife is cleaner than five minutes ago. Good enough.

Thursday, Thanksgiving Day

9 a.m. Abandon plans for fancy appetizers. Decide that if enough wine is plied, raw vegetables will suffice.

9:30 a.m. Distract husband with chopping celery so he does not set table, like last year, using colorful drinking cups and placing butter on Little Mermaid plate.

9:45 a.m. Inside red pepper find green spots. Festive? Moldy? Why has the God of Martha Stewart forsaken me?

10:15 a.m. Remove drinking glasses from cupboard and hold up to light. Realize that cannot see hand on other side of glass. Dim lights further.

10:30 a.m. Realize forgot to clean house.

10:35 a.m. Decide that "clean house"—like "clean knife"—is relative term.

11 a.m. In lieu of centerpiece, throw Beanie-Baby turkey in center of table.

5 p.m. Success! It's over! Remembered dinner rolls in oven *before* burning smell reached dining room. Huzzah! Also thankful we did not repeat Salmonella Bird of 1997; all guests left the house ambulatory.

Plus let's not forget the greatest blessing of all: weight-reducing pecan pie!

Holiday Shopping For the Man of Few Needs

What do you get for Christmas for a man who wants nothing? A man who needs nothing? A man who owns almost nothing (and likes it that way)?

Nothing, right?

See, you think the way I do!

But my husband thinks differently. He thinks that what you get such a person is a "surprise."

Well, surprise! I have no idea what to get him.

This situation is not unusual. In fact, I face this dilemma every Christmas. It is hard to buy anything for my husband because the man has all the worldly needs of a Tibetan monk.

"Do you need clothes for Christmas?" I'll ask him.

"No," he says, looking down at what he's wearing. "I've got these."

"How about skis to replace the pair you've had since 1972?"

"They work fine."

"Perhaps a book?"

"Has the library closed?"

"A new briefcase?"

"Too expensive."

"Power tools?"

"Too dangerous."

"What then?"

"I don't know," he shrugs. "Surprise me."

He does not understand how such a phrase can jeopardize his marital bliss.

It gets worse. Not only does the man reject the idea of adding to our worldly possessions, but his greatest joy in life is throwing things away. Nothing makes him happier than tossing leftovers out of the refrigerator or eating the last granola bar so he can dispose of the box. He empties file drawers in a single dump, cleans out kid's toy chests when they aren't looking, and donates to the Salvation Army any clothing we haven't worn in the past six months.

His favorite day of the week is trash day. Leaving those overflowing barrels on the curb and returning home to find them empty gives him a warm, fuzzy feeling inside.

So, what *do* you give a man like this for Christmas? A gift certificate for a trip to the dump?

"What about hobbies?" a friend suggests helpfully. "Does he collect anything?"

Collections? Are you kidding? Why would he need two of anything? Recreational activities are no help, either. As a long-distance runner, he requires less specialized equipment than your average exotic dancer.

So, what's a well-meaning spouse armed with a Visa card to do?

Sigh, mostly. And think (as all spouses do, and not just during the holidays), "If only he could be more like me!"

You see, in contrast to my husband, I make no secret of my Christmas desires. My list of wants and needs is so long I have to prioritize, then categorize, then alphabetize. I casually point out gift ideas on TV commercials, flag key pages in catalogs, direct his attention to appropriate billboards. I cut out items from advertising fliers and tape them to the TV remote.

And yet, each year, what does my husband buy me?

A surprise.

Now, to give him credit, not all his surprises are as—well—*surprising* as the lime-green V-neck cardigan of 1989, the gigantic moose slippers of 1995, and the humane mouse trap of 1998. Some, like the Victoria Secret sleepwear of 1991, 1992, 1993, 1994, 1995, 1996, 1997, 1998, and 1999, I even wore a few times.

On the other hand, none of these items made it to even the fifth page of my list—a page labeled, "Low priority, nonessentials, Q to Z."

Still, at least I give him a list to choose from. He offers not even a Post-it.

"Buy him what he buys for you," suggests a friend. "That's usually a clue to what people really want: what they give to others."

"He wants a Victoria Secret nightie?"

"No, he wants what he always gets you: he wants a *surprise!*"

I consider this idea anew. Perhaps I can do this. I can look for something along the lines of the surprises he has given me—something, say, in lime green, or sporting felt antlers, or providing a humane escape strategy for small rodents.

Something so unappealing that within two weeks after Christmas, he'll be completely justified in carrying it out to the street corner with the trash.

Perfect! Why didn't I think of this before? The disposable gift!

It's what he's wanted all along.

Overexposed: Our Quest for the Perfect Holiday Photo

We all know the challenge of family picture-taking: how in July of each year, we start trying to take that perfect family photo for the holiday card—and still end up with nothing by late December.

This year, though, I was feeling a bit smug. I thought I had this family picture-taking business nailed.

Just last year, after all, we had managed a stunning family photo. Perfect. No one's finger was in a nostril, no one was examining her navel, no one's fly was undone. Not a single child was showing her underwear.

Not only that, but the photo told a story. In it, the four of us are sitting atop Mount Mansfield, Vermont, looking wind-swept and outdoorsy. Our cheeks are ruddy from the exertion of our exhilarating climb.

Of course, what the photo told about us was not, technically speaking, true. I mean, you couldn't tell from the photo that we had actually driven the car up Mount Mansfield and only hiked the final 100 yards.

In our defense, though, those last 100 yards were steep. My ruddy complexion resulted from holding my 5-year-old by the belt buckle as she scrambled up the face of this cliff, all the while screaming at my husband that there was no way a preschooler was climbing to the top of this thing.

My husband's complexion became ruddy from the several colorful expressions he yelled back.

The kid's ruddy complexions were from dying of embarrassment.

But in any case, it was a great photo, and well worth the 30 hours of family counseling that followed.

We sent the photo as a holiday card to our friends, and many of them hardly even recognized us. "Are you sure that's you?" they asked, "sitting with your preschooler on the edge of a cliff?" They thought we had pasted our faces on a photo of the Von Trapp family. I couldn't have been more delighted.

So, this holiday season, still confident from last year's success, I had a different vision of the whole holiday photo idea.

In fact, I could picture our family in holiday photos for the next several years: forming skydiving rings, scuba diving near sunken Spanish galleons, bungee jumping en famille.

Friends would recognize our cards immediately and exclaim: "Oh, those Crochieres! Always off on some adventure!"

That was my vision, anyway.

In reality, no amount of adventurous vacationing or visual splendor could save us from ourselves.

It wasn't for lack of trying. There was the photo opportunity under a gorgeous stone arch in Utah's Arches National Park. Problem: the long, hot hike to this natural wonder made everyone so cranky we couldn't be coaxed into the same frame.

There was also a photo attempt as our family lounged in the hot springs in Glenwood Springs, Colorado, while a light snow fell around us. The deal-breaker in this case? I was wearing a bathing suit.

There was even a last-ditch attempt at repeating history—another hike up wind-swept Mount Mansfield. Problem: "bad hair day" doesn't begin to describe it.

No, this year's family photo was a lesson in humility. Taken after

Thanksgiving dinner, it shows the four of us with belts loosened, faces bloated, eyes nearly shut from the sleep-inducing effects of turkey and mashed potatoes, sinking contentedly into my mother-in-law's couch.

And that wasn't even the worst of it. When we sent the Christmas card to our friends, they all recognized us immediately.

Christmas and the Frugal Man

My husband has "issues" with the whole idea of holiday giving.

It's not the actual giving itself. In truth, he is a very giving person. However, not when it involves:

a) Spending money. The very idea tries his profoundly Scottish soul.

b) Purchasing items that are not necessities—that is, things you can't eat, find shelter beneath, or use to unclog the bathroom sink.

So, he spends the month of December in deep conflict with himself, paralyzed by opposing desires to give generously and to avoid interacting with an ATM machine.

I spend the month of December trying not to clobber him.

The issue usually comes to a head sometime on Christmas Eve, when he finally decides that he wants to buy our children something "from him."

"No," I assure him, throwing my back against the closet door to try to hold in all the gifts I have already purchased "from us." "Trust me— they're good."

"But there's nothing from *me*."

"If by 'from me' you mean that there is nothing that they are going to roll their eyes at, shove under the far corner of their bed, and never look at again till they leave home for good, then *yes*, there is nothing from you."

Gentle reader, you will think I am being uncharitable here, but bear with me for a moment. You see, "gifts from Dad" tend to be unique. They fall under just a few different categories.

1. That Which Is Practical. Since teenage girls, by definition, already have more clothes than my husband believes any city of 10,000 people should have, they never, in his eyes, "need" clothes. However, there are a few exceptions to this rule. For example, in his worldview, you can never have too many pairs of white socks (in 8-packs from Walmart). You can just imagine the excitement this gift engenders on Christmas day.

"I really like the yellow stitching across the toes this year, Dad," my younger daughter will offer, in the spirit of the day. My husband beams.

Ear muffs are also a favorite of his, though I'm pretty sure they went out of style 30 years ago and my daughters would rather move to Siberia than be seen wearing them. His ultimate gift, however, is long underwear. Each of us owns it in a variety of colors and styles: cotton, silk, polyester. Still, every year, on Christmas Eve, he will ask, "Do you think the girls have enough long underwear?" It's remotely possible that, at this point, he is joking, but you really can't be sure.

2. That Which Is Educational. In addition to clothes-they-will-never-wear, books-they-will-never-read are among my husband's favorite purchases for our children. I'm not talking about frivolous romance or fantasy titles, of course, but books with titles like *How to Improve Your SAT Scores* and *The Organized Teenager*. The book he gave them on *Choosing the Best College* might have been fine, if he hadn't given it to our daughters when our eldest was five.

3. That Which Promotes Fitness. My husband will buy the girls sports paraphernalia, but only if their current equipment is outgrown, broken, or certifiably dangerous. Make no mistake: just because an item is hideous or so outdated that it has no business existing in the

21st century doesn't mean it needs replacing. So what if a child's hand-me-down skis are 6 feet long with 20-year-old bindings and safety straps? They can still make it to the bottom of the hill, right?

4. That Which Is Simply Inexplicable. There's really no category under which you can put the bat house of Christmas 1998. I think its purpose was to drive away mosquitoes. (Or, perhaps, to provide our children with outdoor pets?) In fairness, he only gave it to the girls for Christmas because I warned him, in advance, what would happen if he gave it to me. He's frugal; not foolish.

So, "gifts from Dad" have, over the years, become a special part of our family tradition and lore. We treasure them as conversation pieces, use them to fill all that empty space under the beds, and occasionally, wear them to keep our toes warm.

This December, interestingly, my husband started his holiday shopping early, returning home with a few of the usual items. "Just so they remember they have a father," he muttered.

"Trust me, honey," I assured him. "They know."

How to Parley for Valentine's Day

Around Valentine's Day, negotiations in our household become more complex and multi-layered than your average Arab-Israeli summit.

The "talks" begin about a week before the event—or right around the time that supermarket shelves become so saturated in red that one can spend hours trying to locate a jar of maraschino cherries.

My husband usually opens the negotiations. He'll remark that February 14 is approaching and offer, tentatively, "Do you want me to get you anything?"

"No," I reply. "I'm good."

This is, of course, the desired answer. It's all the man can do to keep from pumping his fists and doing one of those little dances that wide receivers do in the end zone. At this time of year—like no other—he is convinced he married the right person.

But his jubilation is always short-lived, and the reason is simple: Deep down, he doesn't really believe me. He is convinced that this response may be a trick.

Truly, I am not trying to trick anyone. I see Valentine's Day as a holiday for the young, or at least the newly-in-love. When you've been married for decades, you don't really need a Hallmark card expressing your partner's undying devotion; you just want him to take the laundry out of the dryer when it buzzes.

In addition, the traditional Valentine's Day gifts are problematic for me.

Chocolate is lovely, yes; but as a Lindt addict living in a house of brownie-making enablers, I just can't go through the withdrawal thing one more time.

Flowers are pretty, but they die so quickly, and I'm always the one pulling out their slimy stems and dumping out the dirty water, and what kind of metaphor is that for any relationship? (Accurate, some might say.)

And jewelry...well, let's just say that most women are better off choosing it for themselves.

Now, if the traditional gift for Valentine's Day were, say, an iPad, that would be a different matter. But, as far as I know, no one has brought that offer to the table.

So, I'm good. Really.

Except that my husband doesn't believe me.

"Valentine's Day is Monday," he'll note a few days before, adding nervously, "We've agreed we aren't getting each other anything right?"

"That's right," I say, as emphatically as possible. Nevertheless, I can tell he is reviewing his fall-back plans: places where he can get chocolate in a pinch, should he need it.

My husband does not think I'm lying, exactly, but he can easily believe that I may change my mind and simply neglect to tell him. This is not unprecedented in our relationship. No doubt, he fears arriving home on Valentine's Day to an elaborate candlelit dinner with champagne and caviar and cloth napkins in the shape of waterfowl. He knows for a fact that men who find themselves empty-handed in such situations can fail to enjoy the evening to the fullest extent possible.

I do know that on Valentine's Day itself, he will call me on his cell phone as he leaves the office, and check in one more time: "I'm on my way home, and I've taken you at your word, and bought you nothing."

"Great!" I'll reply with enthusiasm. "Same here!"

Granted, it's not everyone's ideal for Valentine's Day, but if you think about it really carefully, there's something touching about a man who makes that one last call to be sure he's gotten me exactly what I want.

That, and taking the laundry out of the dryer when it buzzes, might just buy him another decade or two.

Of course, an iPad would cinch the deal.

Quiz: How's Your Summer Vocabulary?

Are you ready for summer? I mean, *really* ready?

Preparing for summer involves more than just opening your pool, stockpiling tubes of sunscreen, and trying to imagine where that extra five pounds of "winter" will settle when stuffed into last year's swimsuit.

No, real summer prep is more complicated than that. Believe it or not, summer involves a lot of terminology—words that we don't hear other times of the year and are therefore liable to forget, like "sun" and "warmth" and "navel ring."

Here's a quick quiz to see if, perhaps, you are not quite as ready for summer as you think you are.

1. You hear on the radio that it is time to start thinking about your annuals. You:

    a. Make an appointment with your gynecologist.

    b. Call the man who pumps your septic tank.

    c. Both a & b, carefully marking your calendar so as not to confuse the two appointments.

2. You overhear a friend talking about her Caribbean vacation and mentioning a "tankini." You wonder if a tankini is:

    a. A mini armored vehicle with good gas mileage.

    b. A new rectangular-shaped pasta garnished with tropical fish.

c. One of those hybrid bikini-swimsuits that allows the mature woman to use the restroom without training as a gymnast.

3. During a local baseball game, a fan standing near you uses the term "suicide squeeze." You wonder if he is referring to:

a. What your child is doing with the ketchup bottle at the concession stand.

b. How you feel as you try on last year's tankini.

c. The unfortunate move your spouse makes when he thinks you have forgiven him for forgetting Mother's Day.

4. In shopping with your mother, she informs you that she needs some new thongs. You:

a. Hope like heck she is using that old-fashioned word for flip-flops.

b. Steer her towards Williams Sonoma to see if perhaps she is mispronouncing "tongs."

c. Resolve to avoid a beach trip with her and her new Italian boyfriend.

5. The woman at the pool supply store tells you that before you can swim in your newly opened pool, you need to "shock it." You wonder if she is suggesting that you:

a. Toss a hairdryer into the deep end.

b. Announce that bathing suits are optional this year.

c. Explain to the pool how it got all those little tadpoles under its cover.

6. Your husband suggests that the noises you are hearing outside your bedroom window at night are only the "spring peepers." You:

a. Contact the authorities to report backyard "peeping."

b. Turn on the floodlights to see if any of these so-called peepers are cute.

c. Look up the term in a dictionary and ponder why it is the frogs who are having all the fun.

Pencils down. How did you do?

You can score your answers as follows:

Mostly "A" answers: You are careful and literal in defining your summer terms, but need to loosen up a bit before hitting the beach.

Mostly "B" answers: You are a bit more creative in your approach to summer and with further effort, could learn to commune with the spring peepers.

Mostly "C" answers. Bring on the navel ring! You are ready, baby!

So Many Reasons to Celebrate

There's just no pleasing some people.

Recently I went on a personal crusade to educate the public about lesser known spring holidays and celebrations. For example, while most people are familiar with Valentine's Day and Ground Hog's Day, few know that February 1st is "Serpent Day." Nor are they aware that March 3rd is "What if Cats and Dogs Had Opposable Thumbs Day," or that June 15th is "Justice for Janitors Day." (And no, I am not making any of this up.)

To my amazement, however, instead of being grateful for this information, readers complained! Sure, they said, they were delighted to know that February is "Sinus Pain Awareness Month" or that March 13th is "National Open an Umbrella Indoors Day" (celebrated, perhaps, concurrently with "National Poke Your Eye Out Day"?); however, they wanted to know about these observances in advance—to have more time to prepare. Had they known, for example, that June 15th was "Mortician's Day," they surely would have sent flowers. And how could they properly celebrate "National Radon Week" without throwing a party in the basement?

I do sympathize on some level. For example, if you had advance warning that February 4th is *both* "Stuffed Mushroom Day" and "Thank a Mailman Day," you might enjoy the economy of thanking your mail carrier with a stuffed mushroom. (And your mail carrier might feel grateful that his celebration didn't coincide with "Serpent Day," instead.)

So, I've decided to be more proactive and alert people to these special holidays. For instance, an interesting one takes place annually on my birthday, July 27. It is called "Take Your Houseplants for a Walk Day." (Really, I am not making this up.) The website for this special day insists that "strolling with one's plants allows them to enjoy the world about them that they don't enjoy throughout the year." I'm pretty sure that, for those who participate, this celebration is closely followed by "National Lock Me up Day." (Okay, I did make up that one.)

Other summer celebrations include "National Clown Week" (August 1-7), "Romance Awareness Month" (for people who aren't aware they are in a relationship??), and "Moon Day" (July 21st), which sounded a lot more interesting before I realized they were using "moon" as a noun.

September, though, includes some really unique celebrations. The first Wednesday is "Fight Procrastination Day," whose name I find terribly confusing. Does it mean that on this day, people *avoid* avoiding things? Or does it simply mean, "I'll put off that fight until next week." Either way, it sounds like a cause I could get behind.

Other special days in September include:

September 15th—"Marriage Fidelity Day." This is now a *day*?

September 19th—"Talk like a Pirate Day." Apparently, this celebration is quite popular online, though I don't see it gaining a foothold outside of cyberspace. There's a limit to how many "Arrrrrr"s and "Avast ye maties" you can work into your daily conversation without endangering your career advancement.

September 22nd—"Elephant Appreciation Day." Could be worse. At least it's not "Walk like an Elephant Day."

October offers some good choices, as well. For instance, October is:

"Liver Awareness Month." This is great: We all should be aware of our livers. I'm just concerned that spleens around the globe are going to feel slighted.

"Dinosaur Month." On the other hand, I'm not sure how much dinosaurs are going to appreciate this recognition. Too little, too late, and all that.

"Pickled Pepper Month." Does this include a special day for Peter Piper? And if so, what about Little Tommy Tucker and Wee Willie Winkie? And Sally, who worked so hard selling sea shells by the sea shore?

"Pregnancy and Infant Awareness Month." Agreed, it seems very important that, if you are pregnant or have an infant, you are aware of these conditions.

"Sarcastic Awareness Month." Really?

October also includes some special days and weeks, including:

"Nephrology Technologist Week" (2nd week in October). Well, thank goodness! I've thought for years that these people deserved their own week!

"Pet Peeve Week" (same week). I wonder if anyone's pet peeve is nephrology technologists?

"Love Your Body Day" (October 19th). No specifics on how this is celebrated.

Perhaps most importantly of all, I have discovered that September is "Be Kind to Editors and Writers Month." Now, finally, I have found something worth celebrating!

You don't have to send us fan mail or anything, but the occasional stuffed mushroom is really appreciated.

PART 9

I'm in Shape
(as Long as That Shape is a Rhombus)

Being a Soccer Mom Was Easier from the Sidelines

Earlier this fall, I found myself doing something I swore I'd never do: shouting advice to my daughter on the soccer field. And while the phrase "get the lead out" was meant entirely as encouragement, she let me know she didn't appreciate it.

"You try running out there for an hour!" she shouted back.

It wasn't meant as a challenge, exactly. She never imagined that I would do anything so potentially embarrassing to her. But I called her bluff. I did something potentially embarrassing to the whole family. I joined a women's soccer team.

I had never played soccer before, but, I reasoned, how hard could it be?

This wasn't baseball or golf with those itty-bitty balls you have to hit with some kind of stick. Soccer balls are huge, and all you need to do is kick them. I could do that.

I even asked my husband to coach me on some fancy footwork, which he did for five minutes before game time. I felt totally prepared.

I didn't know that my soccer experience would have nothing to do with touching the ball.

First, all the women on the opposing team moved their legs like the performers in "Riverdance," side-stepping around our team as if we were little orange cones. What's more, they moved at speeds that I believed no mother (whose toddler wasn't about to cross Interstate 495) could move. Clearly, these women had not idled away their time at children's soccer games chatting with other mothers—they had paid attention.

Looking back, I realize that the problem was my whole conception of a league in which most women are over 35.

I thought these women would be like me: women who had given birth—perhaps more than once. Women who were now struggling with knee problems or fallen arches or hemorrhoids. Women who were now holding frozen dinners farther and farther from their face in order to read the microwave times.

I thought these women were raised in the same era I was—an era when girls didn't play contact sports and the average female ball game went something like this:

"Your turn to kick."

"Oh, no, I kicked it last. Your turn, I insist."

Instead, these women on the opposing team were completely uninterested in taking turns. They refused to share, even when I yelled, "Pass it to me, pass it to me!" Clearly, no one had ever defined the term "ball hog" for them. Any time someone on our team touched the ball, those other meanies stole it away and scored a goal. Who taught them manners, anyhow?

And then there was the whole business of falling down. Almost no one from their team fell down, and when someone did, she somersaulted like a little circus acrobat, landing right back on her cleats. On the other hand, when someone on my team fell, she went down like a Douglas fir—and, like any reasonable person, didn't get up until someone came to her with an ice pack and the promise of a cold Michelob after the game.

I don't mean to complain about our injury rate, but I know of Civil War battles in which fewer participants were carried from the field. Our sidelines gave new meaning to the term "fallen women."

Despite all this, I've decided to tough it out for a few seasons. I think the whole "soccer mom" thing has been good for my family.

At first, my daughter saw these women's games as pay-back time. She yelled at me to hustle—the way I do to her. However, when the final whistle blew on that first game and I hobbled off the field, she examined me with alarm. "Are you okay?" she asked tentatively.

As I limped to the car, she moved aside to let me in.

"Oh, no, you go first. I insist," she said.

It made me proud—this show of good manners. Perhaps she will grow to be the kind of soccer player I am.

Limping to the Finish Line: Diary of an Untalented Road Racer

Not all of us can be runners.

After many years of trying, I've reached the conclusion that I, for one, cannot.

Oh, I can run, all right. That's just a matter of putting one foot in front of the other at a somewhat faster pace than while shopping. But actually being a runner is different, unless you choose to ignore defining qualities like speed, form, and endurance.

Still, despite my keen awareness of my own limitations, I traditionally join my husband in running in an early-morning New Year's Day road race called "The Hangover Classic."

Our children have sometimes run in this race, too; however, we've stopped inviting them since they have now reached an age at which they can pull the blankets over their faces and respond, "How can I put this? No!"

I like the New Year's Day race because many of the participants are laboring under severe handicaps that wouldn't be a factor on most other days of the year. Note, for example, the widespread use of sunglasses.

The post-holiday impairment of many runners gives me that edge I'm always looking for. Not that my goal is to win—or even place well—in such races. Let's face it: I stink. But, having said that, I'm not interested in completely humiliating myself, either. No, I just want to get some exercise, be out in the fresh air, and, okay, completely blow past somebody—anybody—who is not hobbling on crutches or about to give birth.

I run in the 5K Hangover Classic, but my husband chooses the 10K race, allying himself with a group of fitness enthusiasts who seem to exist on the very margins of society. Case in point: the men wear skimpy little tights of a style that hasn't been seen in public since Shakespearean times—and really, despite MTV, shouldn't be now.

These 10K runners are serious competitors. If you are running in a race with them and trip and fall, they will step over you and leave you for dead.

Even in the 5K race, there are some decent runners. At the starting line, I avoid getting too close to the front of the pack, where you'll find people who wear very little clothing, even in January, and use words like "splits" and "drafting" and "six-minute miles." This kind of talk—even when I don't understand it—can be discouraging to a "challenged" runner like myself. However, I remind myself that these people will soon blow out their knees and spend the rest of their lives wearing ugly braces and doing a lot of swimming in chlorine pools. Yuck. I'd rather be slow.

I tend to choose my starting spot in the upper third of the pack – not because I've earned it, but because no one will know any better. If you do a lot of hamstring stretches before the start, people assume you are a serious runner. (Hint to the novice: Your hamstring is not in your arm.)

My logic is this: If you're near the front of the pack and a lot of people pass you, you can console yourself that these are the elite runners. However, if you're near the back of the pack, just as many people will pass you, but these are sorry-looking folk, and this can do nothing to help your self-esteem.

So, this year, I chose a spot in front of two older women—one in a purple sweatsuit and one who, I swear, was carrying a purse. I felt certain that I could take these grannies in a fair race.

Here's how the race went:

11:00 a.m. I'm off, leaving the old ladies in my dust. I pick out two high-school age girls with matching brown ponytails and decide to pace myself with them.

11:04 a.m. What in God's name was I thinking? I pick out a 30-something woman and pace myself with her.

11:10 a.m. Sigh. I try again, choosing a guy with a large beer-belly. When he pulls off the course and pukes by the side of the road, I enjoy a much-needed break.

11:15 a.m. My husband has coached me to take long strides, so I stretch out my legs. I appear to be imitating a slow-motion film of a somewhat spastic gazelle.

11:20 a.m. A woman motors by me, doing 50 tiny steps to my every long stride. It is the granny in the purple sweatsuit. Truly, my humiliation is complete.

11:25 a.m. A heavy-breather is approaching behind me, and I am annoyed. If I have to endure the heavy breathing, why can't the breather look like Jude Law? This one looks like John Goodman.

11:35 a.m. I'm convinced I've been running for at least two hours. Suddenly, I spot the finish line ahead, and give my final "kick," as we veteran racers like to call it. As I cross the line and move into the runner's corral, I notice the lady in front of me.

Exhilarated, she is waving her purse.

How Playing Racquetball Teaches You to Swing

I recently endured the worst thing that can happen in a racquetball relationship. I caught my partner playing with another woman.

Oh, I should have seen it coming, all right.

I had noticed that our game had gotten stale. My partner seemed just a little, well, bored. I tried to vary things a little: you know, use some different spins, hit the ball off the back wall—nothing that crossed a line. I mean, I wasn't going to try a three-wall serve! Yet no matter how inventive I became, she no longer seemed interested in playing with me.

In retrospect, I can pinpoint the moment when the real trouble started.

We had just finished a rather lackluster game and were relaxing over a drink (Dasani for her; Poland Spring for me). I noticed that my partner's eyes had strayed to another court, where a woman and man were enjoying a spirited rally.

"Look at her crosscourt pass!" my partner sighed.

"Lucky shot," I sniffed.

"No, she's good. You should try getting down low for shots like that. You could score more points."

I sized the woman up. "Her racquet is bigger," I said.

"That doesn't matter."

"Yeah," I replied sarcastically. "Right."

The next thing I knew, my partner had stopped calling me. When I phoned to ask her to play, she made excuses. "Not tonight," she'd say. "I'm really tired."

Sometimes she would seem annoyed and ask, "Didn't we just play last night?"

"Well, yeah," I would admit. "But you used to like to play three times a week."

"That was when we first started," she said. "I can't do that anymore."

Then came the fateful day, almost two weeks ago. I was supposed to be out of town on business, but had returned home a day early and gone to the gym. There I found them—alone in a court with only their gym clothes and racquets.

My partner was laughing as the woman with the great cross-court pass hit an incredible pinch shot. Tears welled in my eyes. I didn't know my partner even liked pinch shots.

As she turned to slam the ball off the back wall, my partner saw me and dropped her racquet. She quickly exited the court. Her new friend followed, sipping her water.

"I knew it!" I cried. "I knew I wasn't good enough for you!"

"It's not that," she replied hastily. "It's just—we were growing in different directions. I wanted to try some new shots. You didn't want to experiment."

"I let you serve from the other side!" I said. "What else did you want?"

"I still want to play with you," she explained. "I just never said I wanted to be exclusive."

Her friend interjected: "No one has just *one* racquetball partner anymore."

"You stay out of this!" I exclaimed. "I've seen your name all over the locker room walls—on those lists of people 'looking for a game.' Why, you've played with half the people in this gym!"

"That's why I'm so good," the woman smiled, and walked away.

Eventually, my partner and I decided to try some coaching. We found a professional to help us work on the problems with our game. The coach analyzed my partner's backswing and advised me on when it's okay to leave the safety zone.

We're back to playing once a week, taking things slow. We've decided not to be exclusive. My partner occasionally plays with other women and—though this shocked me at first—even a few men. For my part, I've begun to look with more interest at those names on the locker room walls.

I haven't quite mastered a pinch shot yet, but I've learned that in a pinch, you can always swing.

Why I Don't Ski Any More

I never meant to mislead my husband. It's just that there were some things I liked to do when I was 22—when we were first dating—that I no longer like to do now. (I'm talking outdoorsy stuff here—keep your mind out of the gutter.)

One thing I no longer enjoy is downhill skiing.

Actually, it's amazing that I ever liked it, as I didn't have the best introduction to the sport. I learned how to ski when I was 13 which—though it would be hard to pick—was probably the most awkward stage in my life.

I had joined our junior-high ski club with ski equipment that I'm pretty sure my parents had purchased from the Lewis and Clark expedition. Even worse was my outerwear. I wore (truly, I remember this, as will everyone else who was there) a fluorescent yellow quilted jacket and a green hat, the combination of which made me look like a giant pineapple. Under the enormous jacket I had on a turtleneck and two bulky sweaters. I believe my thought process was: if I'm going to fall a lot, I'll need a lot of padding. It wasn't bad thinking, as far as it went.

During that first year of ski club, I probably spent about 10% of the time on my feet and 90% lying prone across the ski slope—often with a ski tip jammed in the snow and one leg pinned under me so I couldn't move. At other times I was able to get up by myself, slide another 20 feet across the trail, and fall again.

One of our teacher-chaperones was a nice guy (no doubt this is why he got saddled with me) named Mr. LaBroad. I don't know what happened to Mr. LaBroad in the 30-plus years since junior high, but if he has gone on to a better place, I'm sure his obituary must have mentioned his "saint-like patience."

Eventually, of course, I did learn to make it down a slope. No one watching me would ever have used adjectives like "poised," "skillful," or even "consistently upright;" however, for a few years, I truly enjoyed skiing.

In recent years, though, the sport has become less appealing. I have come to recognize that there are several things about the ski experience that I don't like:

1. It's cold. Now, call me crazy, but on a freezing winter day, I'm almost never inclined to say, "Hey, know what would make this more fun? Let's go to the top of a mountain where the punishing wind can whip freely across our face and all the moisture inside our nose freezes until our nostrils are pinched shut." For some reason, this plan—as fun as it sounds—is always a distant second in my mind to curling up by the fire with a book.

2. I like control. When I ski, I'm not in control. Sure, I know how to stop…most of the time. But then I hit a patch of ice, or my ski tips start to cross, or I start going too fast. Suddenly, my heart rises to my throat, adrenaline rushes through my body, and I break into a cold sweat. If this happened once or twice a day, I could handle it, but for me, it happens about every 45 seconds. It sort of takes the joy out of it.

3. Other people are skiing on my mountain. I might be fine skiing all day on a slope with a few other people, as I was during my bunny-slope days with Mr. LaBroad, but not when 20 people are crisscrossing my path at various rates of speed. I feel like I'm in a giant game of Frogger, and if I try to cross the slope, the chances are good that my green guts will be littered all over it.

4. People ski into trees and die. If I were to stick with skiing, eventually I would be one of those people. I guarantee it.

5. It costs a lot of money. (Actually, I could care less, but this reason works for my husband.)

Oh, I'm not saying that I'll never ski again—I've been bribed into doing sillier things—but today, for instance, I was happy to let my older daughter (now 22 herself) accompany my husband skiing. I can picture her, racing down the slopes beside him, wind whipping across her face, toes turning blue, and think—as I sit by the sunny window and turn on my space heater—I knew there was a reason I had children.

Women's Soccer: My Goal Is to Survive

On Wednesday nights, I join some friends in playing a game that, in many respects, resembles indoor soccer.

The similarities are as follows: the game is played with a soccer ball, a goalie, and a man in dorky knee socks who calls himself the referee. Also, the women wear shin pads—a lower-leg thickening accessory that in no circumstance will you ever see worn outside the facility. (In fact, I've noticed that women on my team remove their shin pads before exiting to the parking lot, as the only thing worse than being hit by a car when you're wearing tattered underwear is being hit when your legs look fat.)

However, apart from these few similarities, the game's resemblance to soccer quickly blurs. Our indoor arena calls this league "beginner's soccer," but I'm still not convinced that Mia Hamm would recognize the rules.

In beginner's soccer, when we kick the ball, we can't say for certain where it will end up. Sometimes it goes behind us, sometimes it spins off to the side, sometimes it hits an opposing player in the face. Occasionally, it rolls close enough to a player on our own team that we call it a "pass" and give each other a lot of high-fives.

If we're not exactly clear on all the rules of indoor soccer, we're at least aware of the key importance of trying to kick the ball into the goal. However, we occasionally forget the finer points of the game, as when one of our defensive players tried to help our goalie by picking up the ball and handing it to her. We've learned that this is a very bad thing.

There are no qualifications needed to play in this Wednesday night league except a discernible pulse and willingness to wear unbecoming black shoes. Consequently, I fit right in.

For several years prior to joining this team, I played in a noncompetitive soccer league. You might think "noncompetitive" implies "easygoing." I thought so, too, before I signed on. I recalled playing "noncompetitive" board games with my children as preschoolers, and they were pretty low-key; since no one won or lost, the game only ended when a player—usually me, but sometimes the child—fell asleep mid-move.

Apparently, though, the women in this league had a different conception of "noncompetitive." They seemed to believe it meant "a game in which you knock people down." Each week, they came primed for a soccer smack-down and rarely left unsatisfied.

That league was advertised as being for "mature" women, which I took to mean over 35 at the very least. I expected that any younger players would have to display significant handicaps—blindness, for instance, or missing limbs.

But no; as I took my first look at my opponents, I realized, with despair, that the t-shirt I was wearing was older than they were. These women probably thought "stretch marks" referred to the indentations we left on the Astroturf when we stretched our hamstrings.

Not only were these women young, but they clearly had spent the last 10 years training with Cirque de Soleil. As they dribbled, passed and shot the ball (repeatedly, and I have to admit, successfully) they moved their bodies in ways I could only fondly remember.

Oh, who am I kidding? My body never moved in those ways.

So, I'm happy with my new stint in beginner's soccer, where players say "sorry" if they bump into you or stop the game to help you up when you fall. Now, when we slap hands at the end of the match and say "Good game!" I really mean it. Before "Good game!" felt like merely a code phrase for "Thank you so much for not body-slamming me."

And when I return home with shin pads in hand and my daughter exclaims, "Oh, Mommy, did you play soccer tonight?" I can say, with all the conviction in the world: "I think so."

Shaking Things up with Zumba

One thing I have to say about this empty-nesting business: it has inspired me to try new things—regardless of whether or not I can pronounce them.

For example, I recently started taking a fitness class called Zumba. At first, though, I got the name wrong. My gym listed the class on its schedule with an exclamation mark for dramatic effect (ZUMBA!), and without my reading glasses, it looked like "Zumbai" to me. So, I went around mispronouncing it for two weeks. Luckily, none of my friends laughed at me behind my back. Being good friends, they laughed at me to my face.

In retrospect, though, my need for reading glasses and pronunciation help may have been early clues that Zumba wasn't created with me in mind.

Zumba, for those who are not familiar with it, is a dance fitness program set to Latin and international music. And by international, I don't mean Romanian folk songs or Italian opera, but rather music that inspires a lot of fast-paced shaking, shimmying, and other unnatural undulations.

Now I realize that such movements aren't unnatural for *some* people. But on my body, nothing undulates *or* shimmies, and if it does, it's rarely in sync with the music or any other body parts.

I have on occasion done some serious shaking, but that's mostly in the winter, before I can get the heat going in the car.

I blame my inability to shoulder-shimmy or hip-roll on my lack of Latin blood. I believe that people like me, of Scottish descent, were not designed for this type of movement. We hail from a climate where people layer on lots of sweaters and tend sheep. There is no shimmying involved in any of this.

Of course, I might have been more comfortable with sambas, salsa, and shimmies if I had ever taken a dance class, but I never have. My parents let my older sister take dance lessons; however, they sized me up and encouraged me to pursue baton twirling, an activity in which all I needed to move was my wrist.

So, all in all, I came to Zumba with a lot of baggage.

My plan, on entering my first class, was to stand near someone who looked more movement-impaired than I was—perhaps a woman who had just given birth a few days earlier, a guy recovering from double knee-replacement surgery, or anyone nursing a really bad hangover. Seeing none, I quietly took a spot in the back of the room.

Unfortunately, as it turns out, all the dance numbers involve turns to face the back of the room. And in the back of the room, just behind me, were mirrors. So, not only was the entire class now positioned to admire my awkward shimmying and shaking from behind, but—what was worse—I could see them myself. Any hopes I harbored that what I was doing looked (a) coordinated, (b) hot, (c) rhythmic, or (d) in sync with anyone else in the class were instantly dashed.

Still, I kept at it. I was amazed at how the instructor could mambo and shake at speeds that I considered hazardous to one's health. So naturally I was taken by surprise when she changed the music and announced, "Okay, this next number is a *fast* one." I laughed out loud. No one else did. As it turns out, she wasn't joking.

I like to think that I can identify the beat in any musical piece; however, once my muscles became exhausted, recognizing the beat and actually moving to it became completely different issues. By the end of the hour, I was running a bit behind the rest of the class: mamboing left when everyone else was moving right, sashaying into the person next to me, and raising my arms above my head just as everyone else was lowering theirs. It was clear that I was moving to the beat of a different drummer.

Despite all this, I really enjoyed Zumba. It was a great aerobic workout. And after a few classes, I even had a little undulation going on.

Which is great, because with the cold weather setting in, I feel I have a lot of untapped potential in the shaking department.

The Joy of "Pumping It Up"

The idea came to me as I struggled to open a jar of pickles.

I realized that while my Zumba class, with its hip rolls and shoulder shimmies, is great for increasing my aerobic capacity (not to mention—as discussed previously—keeping my ego in check), I needed something more.

I needed a class that would tone muscles, increase strength, and—in short—allow me to open pickle jars without running down the driveway to get help from the Fed Ex guy.

So I tried a class that my gym calls "Pump It Up!" In this class, each person uses a virtual truckload of exercise equipment: a large exercise ball, a medicine ball, resistance bands, a step with four risers, hand weights, a body bar, exercise tubing with handles, and a floor mat. (No, really. We use them all.)

After the first week, I renamed this class "Torture with Toys."

Several minutes at the beginning of each class are devoted to collecting the variously sized balls, bars, and bands. For my first 2 or 3 classes, I raced around the room in a panic, thinking that all the light weights or "easy" colors would be taken before I got to them. As it turns out, I needn't have worried. No one else is interested in the wimpy sizes and colors that I use.

By the time I've collected everything, I'm already exhausted. But then comes the really hard part—keeping all of your toys in one spot.

Everyone else seems able to corral their equipment, but the minute I turn my back, my medicine ball starts drifting away, and when I go to chase it down, my exercise ball rolls off and bounces off the head of some guy innocently stretching on his mat.

I look away. If anyone asks, I never saw that bouncy ball before in my life.

My worst enemy is the resistance band—a huge rubber band that goes around your ankles and makes you walk like you're in a chain gang. Other people seem to slip these bands on and off with ease, but mine invariably gets tangled in my shoe lace or stuck on my sneaker. While everyone else has moved on to bench presses, I'm still hopping around on one leg, trying to get free.

Interestingly, although the people in this class *look* normal, they are all hoisting body bars and doing curls with hand weights far heavier than mine. And unlike me, they're not stopping in the middle of the set, gasping for breath and whispering "You've got to be kidding."

Consequently, I've had to develop some strategies to avoid looking like a complete wimp—or at least buy me some time to control my panting. Should you ever try "Pump It Up!" here's what I recommend:

1. Start each set of exercises late—not because you're a slacker, of course, but because you're carefully examining the instructor's technique in order to imitate it properly. Convey this with thoughtful nods of the head.

2. Wear layers of clothing that you will need to remove during the workout, forcing you to miss several sets of push-ups. If you run out of layers to take off, pretend you're cold and start putting some back on again.

3. Glance at the embarrassingly small number (representing pounds) on the side of your hand weight and feign surprise. "Oh, look at that! No wonder this set has been so easy!" (At this point, you may want to slap your hand to your forehead for effect, but first make sure

that you are no longer holding the weight.)

4. While everyone else is doing sit-ups with the medicine ball, simply turn the ball over and over in your hands, as if fascinated by how it's manufactured. You simply *must* find the brand name so you can order one for home.

5. Take a water break and pause to contemplate the music. Who was the disco queen of the 80s who recorded this song? Tap your index finger to your chin, as if the name will come to you any minute—or just as soon as the inner-thigh work is over.

I find that using these little strategies allows me to make it through the class with a minimum of humiliation. And in just a few weeks, the workout has definitely improved my arm strength. Soon, I should be able to open my own pickle jars.

Which is good, because I've noticed that after he drops my packages, the Fed Ex guy is now running back to his truck.

PART 10

Technology Bytes! My Struggles with Modern Life

And I Say to Myself, "What a Wireless World"

It's fall and kids are back in school. Each day, when the bus pulls away from our driveway, there is much rejoicing.

Nothing loud or raucous, mind you. It's not like I throw on some Bruce Springsteen tunes and dance on the kitchen counter. I am far too mature for that. No, the highest I go is the kitchen chairs.

This fall, though, things have been different. Somehow, it seems like the kids have never left.

Take the first day of school. Less than a minute after I closed the door behind my 14-year-old daughter—barely enough time to even *find* a Springsteen song, never mind climb on a chair—the phone rang.

"I left my math book on the counter. Can you run it out to the bus stop?"

The miracle of cell phones. She was calling me from the end of our driveway.

So, on that first day of school, I toted the math book out to the bus stop, said goodbye again—this time like I really *meant* it—and returned to my long-awaited solitude.

Barely a minute into my bliss, the phone rang again.

"I forgot my flute."

She was now calling me from the bus.

I realized, at that moment, that my days of dancing to Bruce were gone forever. There was a new song playing in my head: "You'll Never Be Alone."

In the modern world of wireless communication, I am never alone.

Don't get me wrong, I owe my life to cell phones. For years, carrying one allowed me to leave my children home together without fear that, away from the sound of my voice, they would damage one another. With cell phone in hand, I could threaten punishment at reasonable rates from anywhere within my calling area.

But there are disadvantages to being always in contact with one's children—the prime one being: they are always in contact with you.

Example No. 1. I am in the bleachers at a high school field hockey game, standing for the National Anthem, and the woman beside me has just jumped into the next row because there is something moving in my purse.

My phone is on "vibrate." This phone has the most vigorous vibrate mode I've ever seen. I know that cell phones are now being designed to serve multiple purposes—camera, modem, music library—but I do wonder what use, precisely, my wireless company has in mind for this model.

I take the call, whisper "hold on" and wait impatiently through "… and the home…of the…brave," all the while wondering what fresh disaster has befallen my family. My 10-year-old is on the line.

"What's up, honey?" I exclaim. "Is everything okay?" The woman next to me—clearly, a founding member of Mothers Against Cell Phones at Field Hockey Games—is glaring.

"I've just been thinking," my daughter says, and there follows a long pause. "A week from Friday, if I get all my homework done early, could Rose sleep over?"

I turn to the glaring woman. "Death in the family," I confide.

Example No. 2. I am in the dressing room at The Gap, trying on a swimsuit.

The air conditioning is blasting and I have goose bumps so large that the suit won't fit. (I'm *convinced* that this is the problem.) The phone rings, and again, it is my younger daughter. This time, she is puzzled by some language arts homework.

"It's hard for me to help you from here," I say, juggling the phone and battling more straps than any bathing suit made for a two-armed woman should have.

"Well, what if I read you the paragraph?" she suggests helpfully.

"Honey," I struggle to explain, "Mommy has no clothes on."

There is a long pause before my daughter asks: "*Where* did you say you were?"

Example No. 3. I am at the field hockey stadium again, but I fear no vibrating handbags; my children are with me. The 10-year-old is in hand, and I am waiting for the older child to join us after her game. Suddenly, I spot her walking toward me, phone on her ear. Within seconds, I am vibrating.

"It's me," announces my daughter.

"I can see you," I respond. "So why are we talking on the phone?"

"We have 250 mobile-to-mobile minutes," she explains patiently. "We'll never use them all."

And they say parents today don't spend enough time talking to their kids!

Clearly, they must not have a good calling plan.

Talking to My GPS

I can't help it. I talk to my GPS.

My mother raised me to believe that when someone speaks to you, you respond. So I have trouble with devices, like the GPS, that talk to me using what sounds like a real—albeit a bit robotic—voice. I feel the need to talk back.

My GPS even has a name. I call her Sheila. Even though she's never been to Australia—well, as far as I know.

I don't talk to Sheila all the time. As you might expect, a lot of what she says doesn't require a response. But I do feel that she deserves an explanation when, for instance, she maps out a long trip for me and I spontaneously change my plans.

"Turn right on Main Street in one-quarter mile," she'll advise me.

"Sorry, Sheila," I'll tell her. "I've decided to take a detour."

"Turn right on Main Street," she'll repeat in that persistent way she has. "Turn right on Main Street," she insists, even as I am turning left.

"It's okay," I reassure her. "I'm just getting a coffee at Dunkin Donuts. I'll get back on track."

But I have thrown Sheila into a tailspin. "Recalculating..." she mutters.

It gets worse when we enter the circular drive-thru, which involves an almost 360-degree series of turns. At that point, Sheila completely loses it.

"Recalculating," she says repeatedly, and I swear I hear a trace of panic in her voice. "Recalculating...Recalculating."

"Sheila, relax!" I demand. "I'm just getting coffee." And then, because I feel bad, "Do you want anything?"

Once my teenaged daughter was riding with me when I had to explain to Sheila why I wasn't taking her directions.

"She doesn't care Mom."

"But I'm confusing her!"

"She doesn't get confused. She's a computer."

"You don't know," I said defensively. "You don't know what it's like to be her."

My daughter didn't respond, but I could see her look nervously from me to the GPS and back. "You're not going to start reading to Sheila, like you did to the pet bunny, are you?"

"Of course not," I replied. "I can't read while I drive."

"Good."

"We listen to books on CD."

I have to admit, though, that occasionally I get annoyed with Sheila. Sometimes she talks too much, and then, at other times when I most need her, she clams up.

For example, she enjoys telling me—several times, no less—to turn right at the end of my driveway. Now, believe it or not, I know how to get out of my own driveway. At least, most days.

However, at other times I'll be driving at night in a strange neighborhood, desperately trying to read street signs, and she'll be completely silent.

"Sheila!" I'll plead. "Talk to me!"

Of course, she always comes through in the nick of time, but it can be a bit unnerving.

Even more unnerving was the time I was riding in a friend's car and suddenly, out of nowhere, I heard that familiar voice: "Turn right on Main Street."

"Sheila!" I cried.

"You know this GPS?" my friend asked.

What could I say? I decided to keep it simple.

"Let's just say that Sheila and I have done a lot of recalculating together."

Of Haircuts and Go-Go Boots and Things We Might "Undo"

Sometimes I envy my computer. It can do so many things I admire.

For example, if I lose something on my desktop, I just hit "search" and my computer finds it for me in seconds. In contrast, if I lose something in my house, I can hit whomever I want, but it rarely helps.

My computer also employs some snappy comebacks that I admire. For example, when things become stressful at the office, I wish I could tell my manager that I've "encountered a problem and need to shut down." Or, when someone is pushing my buttons, I would like to be able to tell that person he has made a "serious, fatal error."

But the thing I envy most about computers is their "undo" function. If only we humans had one of those! Think how our lives would be different.

I picture it working like a rewind button. So, for example, on that middle-school ski club trip that I chaperoned, instead of watching helplessly as my cell phone dropped into the ladies' room toilet, I could hit "undo" and the phone would magically pop back up, clean and dry, into the pocket of my bib overalls. I would avoid not only the unpleasantness of fishing it out of the toilet, but also explaining to several snickering teenage girls why I was madly waving my phone under the hand-dryer.

There are other events in my life I would like to undo—several of them from my own teenage years. One unpleasant memory involves an oral report I did in front of my high-school biology class during which I mispronounced the word "organism." (You can just imagine.) Also, I might try to erase that ugly business of the boy I stalked for most of my sophomore year. Undo, undo, undo.

I asked my girlfriends what they would "undo" if they could. Not surprisingly, their responses fell into three categories: hair, fashion, and boyfriends.

My friend Barbara would undo some unfortunate hairdos. There was her high school photo (Prince Valiant) and her wedding hairdo ("Farrah's less attractive sister"). Then there was the whole era in which, as she describes it, "I was trying to look like Andie MacDowell but ended up looking like Andy Kaufman." It was all capped off, so to speak, by the haircut she got after the birth of her second child: the easy-care "man cut." She wonders whether the "undo" function would be able to erase things permanently immortalized in Kodachrome.

Almost all of us who lived through the 1970s have clothing choices that we wish we could undo. For me, it was the enormous red-flowered bell bottoms and the purple suede go-go boots. (Though—thank heaven for small mercies—I don't believe I ever wore the two together.) For my friend Beth, however, the 70s provided the backdrop for the worst fashion nightmare of her life: the day in middle school when, desperate to be part of the latest fad, she wore her floor-length nightgown to school, thinking it would pass as a maxi dress. "The moment I walked into school," she relates, "the first person who saw me asked why I was wearing my nightgown. Needless to say, it was the longest day of my life."

Even as adults, though, we make choices we might later wish to undo. Take the experience of my friend Mary, who tried to test the mettle of a date she found "rather full of himself" by letting her over-protective Cocker spaniel loose when the fellow arrived to pick her up. Of course, she never expected that the dog would make him cower in the stairwell. (Undo.) She *certainly* didn't anticipate it biting him on the hand—or drawing blood. (Undo, undo.) And—worst of all—she *truly* regrets that she couldn't stop from laughing. (Undo, undo, undo.)

Yes, there are many things in life that we might "undo" if we had a computer's capabilities. Since we don't, I guess we need to look on the bright side: at least we don't have a computer's memory.

The Cost of a Free Phone Upgrade

As a rule, I don't like to replace things—cars, appliances, computers, husbands—once I get used to them. As a friend of mine likes to say, "If you think the next model is going to work better than the one you've got, you're kidding yourself."

Recently, however, I've been having problems with my cell phone. The button you push to dial 3 stopped working, and it's been getting pretty tricky to work around that. Even my more creative solutions have failed. For example, I learned that if you try pushing the buttons for 2 + 1, you don't get 3, you get Thailand.

So, when my wireless company called to offer me a free upgrade, I was open to the idea of a replacement. However, the phones at this company's retail store looked nothing like my old one. Instead, the salesperson showed me a series of multi-colored, sleekly designed models that could do anything you ask short of making toast.

"Why can't I get a replacement phone that's just like the one I have?" I asked.

"Well you *can*," he said, shrugging his shoulders to imply he didn't know what kind of moron would make such a choice. "If that's what you want."

"Why wouldn't I *want*?"

The salesperson glanced sideways at me and sighed; he realized that he was going to have to start at the very beginning. "Well," he said, "what do you want your phone to do?"

"Pardon?"

"What is it," he repeated more slowly, "that you would like your phone to do?"

I replied, even more slowly. "I...want...it...to...make...phone...calls."

He paused to consider this response. It appeared that he had never heard it before.

"Then you want the kind you have," he concluded.

For a split second, I thought I had won, but no—he had just refocused. He turned to my daughter, who was also due for an upgrade. She was lovingly caressing one of those multi-purpose, expensive phones that come in different colors to match your outfit.

At that moment, I knew I was, well, toast.

By the time we were done picking out her phone, my surrender was complete. I had allowed myself to get talked into buying a sleeker (read: more expensive) phone that I don't even like as much as my old model.

Oh, sure, all the buttons work, so I now can use the number 3 when I dial—though in truth, I think that's why I'm a little sad.

I miss all the friends I was making in Thailand.

Modern Life Provides Me with
Too Much Information

A few weeks ago, as I waited for an elevator in my office building, I noticed two repairmen working in one of the adjoining elevators. The men looked puzzled. In fact, they looked stumped.

What really alarmed me, though, was when one guy looked at the other, shrugged, and asked, "Super glue?" His friend nodded.

This was way more information about elevator repair than I needed to know.

Personally, I've always preferred to believe that some things operate by magic. Although I realize that this belief is not grounded in science, I figure that it's no worse than other unscientific theories currently worming their way into our schools' science curricula. Like those perspectives, my theory saves me from having to worry about a lot of inconvenient facts.

When things work by magic, you don't have to think about individual nuts and bolts, cables, or circuits. You don't have to worry about what happens When Switches Go Bad. And you don't have to consider how many problems in this world are solved through the application of a little super glue.

My magic theory applies not just to elevators, but to other modes of transportation, including—though not limited to—automobiles, airplanes, escalators, and roller coasters. I really don't want to know how they work.

Flying, in particular, is something I find best thought of in terms of magic. (By "flying," of course, I'm referring to traveling on an airplane. Flying on your own really IS magic.) Yet, despite my desire to travel in technological ignorance, airline personnel seem determined to keep me informed about matters that I feel are none of my business.

Just last week, for example, as I was about to board a shuttle to New York, a voice over the intercom announced that passengers from my flight should move to a different gate, because our plane was experiencing "possible mechanical difficulties."

"Possible?" I smile pleasantly at the woman behind the desk. "You mean, like, you're not really sure?"

She didn't actually respond, but she did take note of my height, hair color, and clothing and handed it to the flight attendant, whom I could tell was already mentally denying me my complimentary pretzels.

I'm sorry, but for me, "possible mechanical difficulties" calls up an image of those two repair guys, this time examining a large section of broken airplane wing, shrugging, and asking each other, "Super glue?"

See what happens when you provide people like me with too much information?

How hard would it have been for the airline to direct us to another gate by saying, "We're giving you a better view of the luggage handling"?

Instead, the assault of unwanted information continued.

As we passengers shifted to the new gate, we had a full view of the front of the aircraft. As I watched in amazement, the pilot opened his side cockpit window, sat on its edge, and proceeded to clean the outside of the windshield with a cloth.

I found this scene alarming on at least two levels.

First of all, those windows *open*??? I could have lived my whole life in happy ignorance of this fact.

Second, isn't there a more technologically advanced way to clean the airplane windshield? A system of wipers and washer fluid comes to mind. It works in my car. I mean, what happens if that windshield needs to be cleaned *during* a flight?

Suppose our plane suddenly bears down on a flock of migrating geese that hasn't enjoyed a pit stop in hours. How much, um, fuel would they have to discharge to completely obscure the pilots' vision?

I don't know the answer to any of these questions, but if you do, please keep them to yourself.

Clearly, I already know too much for my own good.

PART 11

Secrets and Shames

Someone Is Watching My Chocolate

A lot of people are spooked by the amount of surveillance that takes place in our society. Until recently, though, I wasn't bothered.

I don't mind being videotaped as I walk through parking lots. I think of it as having my own reality show. I imagine the camera angles, hear the background music playing, walk with an air of confidence, and then realize how stupid I look when I can't find my car.

Neither am I bothered when people take my picture for a license, passport, or gym membership. At least, it never used to bother me when the photo was of me and just one chin.

I'm even good-natured about security measures in airports, although I feel my family has often been unfairly singled out for surveillance. Until our country is attacked by a gang of freckle-faced, middle-school terrorists, I think they could stop wanding my kids.

In general, though, I haven't spent a lot of time fretting about issues of privacy versus surveillance.

Recently, however, a receipt from my local pharmacy has made me rethink this casual attitude.

At the bottom of the receipt, after noting the total number of prescriptions I have filled so far this year, they listed—are you ready for this?—my *year-to-date purchases of Hershey candy bars.*

That's right: I have had to face the stunning realization that someone out there is tracking my chocolate habit.

To me, this crosses a line. Take my photo; peer inside my purse; confiscate my nail clippers if you must. But the relationship between a consenting adult and her Hershey bar—with or without nuts—should be a private matter.

I say this even though my year-to-date chocolate total was nothing to be ashamed of. Only eight chocolate bars in the first four months of the year is a fairly clean record—one I'd be willing to share with my Godiva 12-step group.

But it does leave several questions unanswered. Like *why* is this store tracking my chocolate?

Is it for my own protection? When I give the cashier my special pharmacy card, does my photo appear on her computer screen with the words "chocolate addict" stamped across my face? And is it accompanied by instructions to "substitute carob whenever possible?"

Perhaps this warning system prepares the store employees for chocolate-related emergencies. It might include some tell-tale signs of trouble, like "pupils enlarge when entering Easter candy aisle" or "hands shake when purchasing Whitman Sampler."

Or, is their chocolate surveillance merely a marketing ploy, designed to exact more money from the already desperate? Does the little asterisk next to my photo instruct the clerk to "push the Lindt truffles with this one?"

The whole situation gives me the creeps. I have to wonder: If they are monitoring my chocolate habit, what else might they be tracking? Many of my purchases could require explanation…I mean, context.

For example:

Sure, I bought three People magazines during consecutive weeks this spring, but I needed to keep tabs on whom George Clooney was dating. This information was vital to the appropriate channeling of my fantasy life.

Yes, I purchase a lot of sneaker spray, but before you remove me from your beach party list, keep in mind my marathon-training, soccer-playing, cross-country running family. Clearly, *my* sneakers are not the lion's share of the problem.

I'll admit that I've bought several pairs of "reading" glasses in recent months, but does anyone stop to consider that they may be a fashion statement? I enjoy changing my "look" every so often—for example, every time I go to read small print.

Finally, I think it's important to understand that the bunny ears I bought on sale after Easter were for a church function! I swear it!

In conclusion, I need some answers. I want to know exactly who is monitoring my chocolate purchases and why. I want to know what they plan to do with this information. And most importantly, I want to know if they are going to call me when there's a sale on the Lindt truffles.

Ensuring one's privacy is one thing; ensuring one's bliss is another.

Worse than Skeletons in Your Closet: Barbies in Your Basement

You can learn a lot about yourself and your family from examining the contents of your basement. And sometimes, it's stuff you didn't want to know—or have tried really hard to forget.

A recent archaeological excursion into our basement uncovered the artifacts of an almost forgotten time: the Barbie Era. My husband and I vaguely recall this period, when wandering through the house barefoot always resulted in at least one puncture wound from a tiny, pink, high-heeled pump. Not coincidentally, the Barbie Era was marked by the use of extremely colorful language.

In the dark recesses of our basement, I uncovered two large bins filled with pink plastic remnants of Barbie's Dream House, Barbie's Dream Bed, Barbie's Dream Camper, Barbie's Dream Spa, etc. I seem to recall that each of these items was purchased at great cost, assembled with great frustration, and fell apart within the first hour of use. How lucky, though, that we saved all the parts!

More unsettling, however, was the multitude of smaller artifacts I found among the ruins. Specifically, in the two bins, I counted no fewer than 67 (that's right—67) tiny combs and hairbrushes and exactly 24 hand mirrors, not mention two tiny hairdryers that still made whirring noises when you pushed the button.

I was stunned. What subtle influence might all this cosmetic paraphernalia have had on my young, impressionable daughters?

I flashed back to the time that our family hiked up Mt. Washington, when my older daughter was 12. Somewhere near the summit I had discovered that, although my daughter had packed no food or drinking water, she somehow had found room in her small backpack for 3 different hairbrushes. My jaw had dropped as she explained: "Well, this brush is for tangles, and this one is for bumps, and—I don't know—I just like this one."

Now, years later, as I rummaged through the pink detritus of my children's youth, I wondered: how else had Barbie influenced them?

I didn't have to wonder for long. The bins held lots of swimwear—always a favorite of my girls—as well as beach towels, sunglasses, and tiny CD players. Of course, lots of kids like the beach, I told myself. It doesn't mean anything. Then I found a tiny aqua surfboard and shuddered. Beside me, propped against the wall, was my 19-year-old's full-sized aqua surfboard.

Instantly I recalled how, just last spring, the players on an opposing soccer team had taken one look at my long-legged younger daughter with her hair in a high ponytail and derisively christened her "Soccer Barbie."

This was getting scary: Barbie had been more of a role model to my children than I had.

I searched the bins in vain for any sign of the politically correct dolls I was certain I had bought them: Policewoman Barbie, Veterinarian Barbie; Astronaut Barbie. Yet somehow all I found were Surfer Girl Barbie, Fashion Model Barbie, Rock Groupie Barbie, and one that, based only on her clothing, I'd have to call Street-Walker Barbie.

I couldn't bear any more. I decided to toss everything before any other lives were affected.

As I filled the trash bags, however, I noticed several bizarre things about these Barbie collections. In one bin, most of the Barbies were either decapitated or had their hair chopped off—sometimes both. I didn't recall my children being into ritualized beheadings (I'm convinced I would have noticed this), which lead me to wonder: What happens when a dozen Barbies are locked in a container for 10 years with one only Ken? I don't know about you, but I'm thinking: *major cat fight.*

The second bin contained a single undressed Ken doll with about a dozen half-clothed Barbies. This seemed more normal, except that there were about 16 Baby Krissy dolls—about a dozen more than I remember us owning. Again, I had to ask: what exactly went on in these bins? Looking at Ken, you wouldn't think it possible—and yet, you wonder… .

In the end, I realized that cleaning the basement had raised too many troubling questions. Some parts of your house, just like some eras in your life, are better left unexamined. Besides, we all have better things to do with our free time.

If you don't believe me, ask Ken.

The Editor's New Clothes

Remember how, some years ago, Michael Jackson created a big hullabaloo when he showed up for a court appearance in his pajamas?

Personally, I sympathized with Michael on this one. As someone who is self-employed and works from home, I find that much of what I wear on a daily basis could be classified as (or used for, or once was) pajamas.

I've worked at home now for 12 years, and I no longer own anything that isn't held together by a drawstring.

Now granted, I have little need for high fashion when my "business meetings" involve admonishing my pet rabbit about keeping her "business" in the litter box. But that doesn't mean I don't suffer from Jimmy Choo-envy. If only people could walk in my furry moose slippers for a while, they would feel my pain.

Imagine what it's like to have your former business-wear labeled as "retro" and sought after by middle-school children for weird dress-up days.

Consider the guilt I feel in looking forward to my daughter's high school graduation because—even though I will miss her when she's at college—I really need a new dress.

My wardrobe dysfunction came to a head recently when I received an invitation to interview for a big-city job.

In all honesty, I can't say I responded well to this fashion emergency. I made mistakes. That's why I'm determined to share what I've learned. Here are some key warning signs that you haven't been paying enough attention to fashion:

- You lay out your three best sweatshirts—the one with the sleeves ripped off; the one with the large bleach stain (but only on the back); and the one that is in pretty good shape but proclaims, "So Many Men; So Few Who Can Afford Me." You ask your husband which one he'd wear to a job interview. He says he'd go for the one with the bleach stain, but only if you accent it with a nice scarf.

- You realize that—apart from the fuzzy moose slippers with felt antlers—every pair of footwear in your closet stopped fitting after you gave birth to your second child.

- You narrow down your choice of "nice" pants by eliminating everything with holes in the knees. What remains is a pair of sweatpants with stripes down the side. You wonder if you could dress them up a bit—perhaps by accessorizing with a leather belt.

- Despite the fact that snow still covers the ground, you are amazed to find nothing at the mall that is not pink, lime green, or pink and lime-green striped. This includes shoes, handbags, and swimsuits. (Okay, you weren't looking for one, but geez, it was on sale!)

- You are puzzled when the salesperson uses the term "dress pants," as this seems like a contradiction in terms. You decide that it describes some new hybrid fashion, like the "skort," only longer. You tell her you'd like to see one. She looks at you oddly, then recalls an emergency in lingerie.

- On the day of your interview, you do not stop to consider that, because you have not worn pierced earrings in the last seven years, you may not be able to simply insert them now without drawing blood.

- You believe that you will be able to remove the blood stain on your new pink and lime-green jacket with soap and water, despite the fact that the label says dry clean only.

- You wonder what you can use to camouflage the soap and water stain on your jacket: perhaps some kind of festive pin? A corsage? Your father's World War II medals?

- You cover your new suit (and blood stain) with a heavy wool coat and scarf. You decline to remove the coat during your interview, leading the interviewer to believe that (1) you don't trust her with your outerwear; (2) you have the body temperature of a reptile; or (3) you plan to flash someone on your way out of the building.

- As you leave the interview, you realize that you have lost a glove. You put on the single glove and reflect, perhaps not for the last time, that Michael Jackson may not have been as far from the mainstream as he seemed.

Return of the Closet Organizer

As soon as he opened the closet door, my husband knew that I had relapsed.

The evidence was right there, for anyone to see: the new shelves; the little green, red, and blue storage bins; the color-coded sticky labels.

"You've been organizing again, haven't you?" he accused.

What could I say? It seemed futile to deny it. After all, his baseball caps didn't arrange themselves by color on their own.

"It started with one cabinet," I confessed. "I thought I'd just organize a few DVDs. It seemed harmless."

"You know you can't stop after one cabinet."

"I was convinced I could handle it," I admitted. "I thought that I could stop whenever I wanted."

He shook his head.

We both knew there are two kinds of organization addicts. Some are compelled to organize every day; others can go long periods of time without organizing, but once they start, they can't stop. I belonged to the latter category.

I had been "clean" for almost two years (clean, in this case, meaning "not obsessively organized"). I had let Tupperware run amok in the cupboards; allowed cascading stacks of towels to rule the closets; and stood by idly while the gadgets in my kitchen drawers had hooked up unnaturally—can openers with glue sticks, measuring spoons with cheesecloth, duct tape with turkey basters.

I had learned to turn a blind eye to disorder. If I found a light bulb in the storage container labeled "batteries," I would leave it there. If the bookcase was overflowing, I would shove in one more paperback sideways and walk away without a single facial tic.

Naturally, some situations tested my resolve. Once, when I accidentally opened a friend's freezer full of neatly stacked and labeled frozen food, I got an organizing rush and almost had to make an excuse to leave.

But I held firm to my goal. That is, until I threw it all away with one trip to Target.

Clearly, I should never have ventured into the section labeled "Home Storage." I knew perfectly well what might happen. I saw the rows of brightly colored plastic containers and I had to have one. Just a little one.

"One won't hurt," I told myself.

But it did. Within a week, I was secretly buying all sizes of baskets and bins, smuggling them into the house, and hiding them in my office. When no one was home, I would organize in places where no one would notice—the laundry room, the cabinets under the sink, the girls' bathroom.

Inevitably, as the addiction grew stronger, I became reckless. When I organized the closet that I share with my husband, I must have known in my heart I would be found out—and perhaps I wanted to be. Among other things, I had started to run out of labels.

So I write this today as someone who has renewed her resolve and is back on the wagon. I'm hopeful that, by making my struggle public, I can help others with this strange, rare affliction.

After all, I've bin there.

My Life-long Quest for Talent

I've noticed that certain annual events tend to make us take stock of our lives.

For some people, it's the start of a new year. For others, it's a birthday or performance review at work. I have one friend who seems to become philosophical each year when her septic tank is pumped ("out with the old; in with the new" and all that). But that's the subject for another column—albeit one I probably won't write.

Personally, I tend to get reflective around the time of our annual church variety show.

I became involved in the variety show about five years ago, which is—not coincidentally—when they stopped calling it a talent show.

Oh, it wasn't like that…exactly. In fact, I was the one who suggested the name change. I wanted to participate and couldn't think of anything I could do that would fall under the broad heading of "talent." To be honest, I couldn't think of anything I could do that would fall under the heading of "watchable."

And this explains why I tend to brood around this time each year. This whole "talent" issue has been a life-long challenge for me.

It all started with my high school's annual variety show, which opened with an enormous kickline. Twenty tap-dancing girls would burst onto the stage, kicking their legs to chin height and dropping into sudden, breathtaking splits. I longed to be one of them, but was fairly certain that for my untrained body, this combination of kicking and splits would impair my future ability to have children, or even exit the building with dignity.

I had similar issues with singing. Only here, the danger was not to myself but to the audience—and probably any dogs within a hundred-yard radius. I just couldn't negotiate the high notes. Even to this day, the song "Happy Birthday" stretches the very edges of my vocal range.

I had only two "talents" as a child. I rarely speak of either of them and you will see why.

One was baton twirling. Apparently, my parents took a good look at their daughter—scrawny, pigtailed, with braces—and decided my prospects in life could only be improved by carrying a big stick.

The other talent, it pains me to confess, was synchronized swimming. To fully appreciate this activity, you have to picture my high-school's modestly cut, army-green tank suits; white bathing caps; and nose clips. You also have to picture my inability to do the splits on stage and transfer that image to performing them upside down in a pool.

Now, some experiences are humiliating at the time and others are humiliating only in retrospect. These experiences were both.

So, in the years since high school, I've continued to search for my special talent. At different times, I thought maybe I had found it. For example, I've considered my potential to be a mime, as evidenced through the variety of silent gestures (pleading, cajoling, threatening, decapitating) I employ to get my daughters off the phone. I've also imagined a talent for acrobatics; after all, I have a proven ability to trip over my husband's shoes in the dark, landing with one knee on the TV remote, turning on "Friends" at 2 a.m.

However, I'm pleased to report that this year, for the first time, I am looking forward to our church variety show, as I have finally identified my true talent:

I stomp.

That's right. I read recently that "stomp" refers to an art form in which the performer produces percussion out of normal household objects. And I said to myself: "Hey, I do that all the time!"

Whenever our family has cardboard boxes that need to be recycled, I flatten them by stomping on them. Clearly, I must be the best stomper around, because no one else in my family seems able to do it; they just toss their boxes in a corner of the kitchen for me to stomp on.

In fact, I've already explored a variation on the usual cardboard-flattening sounds when I mistakenly stomped on a full cereal box that someone had left on the floor after grocery shopping. The sound was exquisite; the Raisin Bran, though, was a little worse for the encounter.

My husband, of course, couldn't let go of the fact that I was now a cereal killer. I just filed it away as another unexplored talent. Who knew?

Dreams of Being a Superhero

When I was a child of 6 or 7, I would occasionally dress like Batman's side-kick, Robin, the Boy Wonder. No joke. I'd put on a red swimsuit and tights and fasten a yellow towel around my neck with a safety pin.

No, really. I have pictures.

I mention this not simply to point out how geeky I was as a child, though this is demonstrably true. No, I raise the issue of my crossdressing past to show that, from a very young age, I longed to be a superhero and help people in need.

I dreamed up dozens of scenarios in which I would, for example, pull a child from a burning building, push someone out of the way of a careening station wagon, or even bring a neighbor important mail that was mistakenly delivered to our house. Sadly, however, throughout my childhood, no clear opportunities for heroism—not even the misdirected letter—presented themselves.

As I grew older, I began to question my qualifications for heroism. I mean, some people act swiftly and courageously in dire circumstances and others stand paralyzed like a deer in headlights. I had a nagging suspicion that I might be less like Robin, the Boy Wonder, and more like Bambi's mother.

My fears were confirmed two years ago when I was teaching my daughter how to drive and she mistook the gas pedal for the brake, driving us into a construction trailer. Now, in my defense, this all took place in the space of 2 seconds. Still, I had to wonder if someone with quicker reflexes might have grabbed the steering wheel or pulled up the emergency brake. Instead, I closed my eyes and yelled, "Ahhhhhh-hhhhhh!" As superhero auditions go, it was not promising.

Since that incident, I've abandoned my childhood ideal of hero-ically saving someone, though I still try to help people in difficult situations when I can. For example, I recently guided a blind man across a complicated intersection in Boston. I nearly killed us both in the process, but luckily he seemed unaware of it. As we parted ways, though, it occurred to me that—just possibly—he might have been better off without my help.

In general, I feel that my skill set might be well suited to helping someone who is lost—perhaps a tourist from another country who is visiting Boston. For instance, what if that person can speak only French? This would be an incredibly convenient coincidence, since that is the only other language I speak. I could be a real hero to that person. Or, at the very least, I could take his photo in front of Faneuil Hall.

Opportunities for assisting lost people occasionally present themselves as I walk to my bus stop in Boston. Just last Friday, a woman hesitantly approached me.

"Can you help?" she asked in accented and halting English. "I look for train."

"You mean the 'T'?" I asked. "The subway?" She didn't understand. "Under ground?" I tried. I made hand motions that were supposed to indicate something subterranean, but probably just looked like I was doing the Macarena.

"Yes?" she replied tentatively. "I think?"

I was delighted. This was right up my alley, so to speak. We were just around the corner from the Copley T-stop, so I motioned for her to follow me and pointed to the other end of the block. She seemed dubious, but I tried to communicate that she shouldn't worry, she'd see the "T" entrance when she got there. I raced off to catch my bus.

Two blocks later, a new thought occurred to me. What if she had meant an *Amtrak* train? Like, for example, the one that was less than half a block from where the woman had been standing? I began hitting myself in the head. Repeatedly. Passersby gave me a wide berth. Here had been my perfect opportunity to help someone in need and I probably had made her predicament worse.

I wondered if someone else would be able help her. Her English had seemed so minimal and her accent so thick. What was that accent, anyway? I knew I could identify it.

That's when I realized: it was French.

For the safety of the world, I'm turning in my cape.

Running on Empty

I'll admit that I have not always been a perfect role model for my children.

Probably this is true in many areas, but it's particularly true when it involves driving, and even more so when it comes to keeping my car's gas tank filled.

I usually wait until the gas gauge's "empty" light turns on before I fill up, but not always. Sometimes I wait longer. After I've driven another 10 miles, said a few Hail Marys, and repeatedly shifted the car into neutral to coast toward stop lights, I generally concede that it might be time to get gas.

My daughters, both drivers now, are far more responsible about fueling up than I am. No doubt their good habits are the result of repeated childhood trauma. ("Hold on, girls! Mommy's going to try to coast into that Sunoco station up ahead.") As the saying goes: if you can't be a good example to your children, at least be a terrible warning.

I hadn't actually run out of gas in decades, but I did recently, and my 18-year-old daughter, who was highly amused by the whole experience, insists that I write about it. Of course, I was highly amused by her close encounter with the construction trailer during her first driving lesson, but she is still not so keen about my telling that story. That's okay. She'll go away to college next year and I can write what I want.

So, yes, I ran out of gas on Interstate 95 a few weeks ago. But it wasn't my fault. The problem *clearly* was the gas light, which didn't bother to come on until we were almost completely out of gas. What good is a warning light that only lights up once your car is empty? That's not a warning—that's an "I told you so." I get enough of those from my husband.

Unfortunately, I noticed the "empty" light flash on just as we passed Exit 3—an exit so far from the next sign of civilization that they should rename it the "You-Really-Should-Get-Off-Here-Stupid" exit. Immediately, I sensed we were in trouble. The memory that flooded back to me—of having glanced at the gas gauge two hours earlier and thought, "Gee, I'd better get gas soon"—was not a good sign.

I don't recall what colorful language I used to express my unhappiness, but my daughter turned off the radio to listen. Teens think they invented this colorful language, but really, they didn't.

I tried nursing along the sputtering car as long as possible in hopes of making it to the next exit, but we soon were reduced to coasting in the breakdown lane and eventually slowed to a complete stop. In case you're ever in this situation yourself, here's a tip: trying to move the car a little farther by putting it in neutral and having both you and your daughter rock back and forth in the front seat doesn't work. Just in case you were wondering.

My problem (well, besides the lack of gas) was that our car wasn't pulled far enough off the road for my comfort. Tractor-trailers whizzed by so close to us I swear I could read the warning on their side mirror. But now I faced a parenting dilemma. One of the most important rules I have always emphasized with my daughter is: If you break down on the highway, do not, under any circumstance, get out of the car.

Luckily, the other rule I've always relied on is, "Do as your mother says, not as she does."

I waited for a moment when no cars were coming for a long stretch, ran out behind our car, and starting pushing it. To my amazement, the car actually moved. However, for some reason, it wasn't getting any closer to the shoulder of the road. As I looked through the rear window, I saw that my daughter, in an effort to help, was once again vigorously rocking back and forth in the front seat.

I knocked on the passenger-side window and applauded her effort. "That's great, honey," I panted, "but one of us needs to steer." My daughter is bright, but sometimes a tad blonde. She gets that from me.

Eventually we succeeded in moving the car a little closer to the shoulder. There, we called my husband who good-naturedly came to rescue us with enough gas to make it to the nearest station.

Which was, I hope, the biggest lesson my daughter learned that day. If I haven't set a good example in any other way, I hope I've taught them this: choose as your life's partner someone really good-natured.

And every so often, allow him to say, "I told you so."

PART 12

To Middle Age…and Beyond

A Mind Is a Terrible Thing to Waste

A few weeks ago, I was chatting with my next-door neighbor when she asked what kind of birds I was seeing at our birdfeeder.

There were several moments of awkward silence before I finally offered: "Little…yellow and black ones?"

Okay—so I don't know birds. I made it through four years of college, but I barely can distinguish between a hummingbird and a turkey.

Nevertheless, I can accept this deficiency in my knowledge. Clearly, I'll never be an ornithologist—so what?

Unfortunately, shortly after the bird incident came the whole flower fiasco.

I decided some color around the front of our house would look nice. So, I drove to the garden store to buy flowers.

"What kind are you looking for?" the flower man asked.

It wasn't an unreasonable question. Nevertheless, it had me completely stumped.

"Um…pretty ones?" I tried.

The man thought I was joking. However, he didn't find the joke particularly funny. Apparently, all his flowers were pretty. What *kind* of pretty flowers did I want?

My eyes darted around the greenhouse. Luckily, I fixed on the perfect answer. "Pink," I said decisively.

The flower man sighed and handed me over to a young sales clerk who, I'm guessing, was their specialist in "pink."

I left that flower store with a profound sense of my own ignorance. I began to notice that other women seemed to know more about these things than I did. Although they were all busy with homes and families and careers, they knew that "annuals" referred to something other than a gynecological exam.

Where had I been? What was taking up so much space in my brain that I thought "phlox" was what I did to my teeth at night before bed? What *did* I know about?

Not math, that's for sure, as anyone can attest who has seen me calculate a 15 percent tip on my fingers.

Not cooking. Unless it comes with instructions clearly printed on the side of the box, I don't attempt it.

Not sports. Until recently, I thought that "March Madness" was a sale.

Not computers, politics, or music. Not art, or carpentry, or how to program the TV remote. Not fashion. Not fishing. Not economics.

I won't go on. The list would just embarrass us both.

It took weeks of self-reflection to figure out what I did know—what information was clogging the neural pathways of my brain so that nothing else was being given security clearance. And in the end, the list was impressive. Indeed, it turns out that I am a veritable fount of knowledge. Here's just a sampling of what I know:

The phone numbers of my children's 15 best friends, their birthdays, and whether they own a pair of softball cleats we can borrow in a pinch.

What everyone in my family, plus these 15 best friends, will eat on a pizza.

The theme songs to "Gilligan's Island," "The Addams Family," "Nanny and the Professor," or almost any sitcom of the 1960s.

Which of my daughters' jeans to never, ever, wash in hot water again.

The Gettysburg Address, "The Rubaiyat of Omar Khayyam," "Casey at Bat," and five other poems I had to memorize in the sixth grade.

The directions to any soccer field within a 30-mile radius, plus the Dunkin Donuts closest to each.

More than I need to know about George Clooney's love life.

Several things that I wish I could forget, including all the words to "The Barney Song" and "Tie a Yellow Ribbon Round the Ole Oak Tree."

Of course, that's not all I know. That's just the most impressive stuff.

They say that knowledge is power. I think they're right. I may not know the difference between a tufted titmouse and a great blue heron, but I know what can happen to a mom who washes a new pair of jeans in hot water. And it ain't pretty.

Remembering Bobby Sherman...
and Nothing Else

A while ago, when I turned 40, friends asked if I planned to write a column about that experience. I replied that I would, as soon as I found something funny about it.

Years later, I'm still looking.

It's not that I'm sensitive about aging. It's just that if one more person utters the word "perimenopausal" in my presence, I'm going to break his nose.

So, perhaps there are some aspects of this aging process that I'm not handling as well as I could. Take yesterday, for example. I completely lost it over the words to a Bobby Sherman song.

Who?

Okay, if you don't know who Bobby Sherman is, you're too young to be reading this column. Go do your homework.

So, anyway, there I was, happily searching the refrigerator, the microwave and the potted plants for any possible place I might have left my car keys, when I found myself singing Bobby Sherman's hit song, "Easy Come, Easy Go."

I'm takin' the shade, outta the sun,
Whatever made me think that I was number one?
I oughta know: easy come, easy go.

Now, you may not understand why this is so upsetting. After all, I remembered all three verses plus the bridge of an eminently forgettable pop song by a largely forgotten teen idol of the late '60s. That's not bad for someone who is peri…I mean, over 40, right?

But the point is: I could remember all the words to this Bobby Sherman song, *yet I still couldn't recall where I put my car keys.*

It gets worse. The more I thought about it, the more I realized that my mind is completely clogged with useless trivia from my youth. I can sing the theme songs to "The Brady Bunch," "F Troop" and "Mr. Ed." I know Peter Tork's real name and where Davy Jones was born. I know more than any normal, well-adjusted person should know about The Captain and Tennille. I know all these things and yet, sometimes, I can't bring to mind the name of my first-born child.

"You! Tall blonde one!" I have to yell.

I hear the tall blonde one mutter to her sister, "I like it better when she calls me your name."

"Yeah, well don't assume this is age-related," I bellow. "My memory is fine. I know all the words to a Bobby Sherman song."

"Who?" they ask in unison.

Like I need this sort of grief.

I lost my mind and fell apart
I had to find myself in time
Now I can start all over again

What irks me is this: Clearly, anything I learned between the ages of 9 and 12 is stored in permanent memory. I will never lose it, no matter how hard I try. Even lyrics that make me cringe like:

So happy to find I still can smile
And dig the show

And what bothers me most about all this is the lost potential. It occurs to me that if they had put the complete works of Shakespeare, the Bhagavad Gita, or the entire U.S. Constitution to a Bobby Sherman tune, I would know those things. Instead, what fills my mind is:

Sittin' it out, spinnin' the dial
Just thinkin' about the chump I've been I have to smile
Didn't I know?

The phone rings. I can't remember where I left it, but eventually find it in the refrigerator. I answer it.

"You forgot to pick me up after soccer practice again."

"I did?"

"Yes."

"Oh," I reply. "Who *is* this?"

There is an audible sigh on the other end. "The tall blonde one."

"OK, I'll come get you. One more question?"

"Yes?"

"You don't happen to know where I put my car keys?"

Easy come, easy go.

The Curious Case of the Missing Pants

Have I mentioned that I've become a little flakey in my middle age?

I thought it was bad enough when I had to check whether the bristles on my toothbrush were wet to see if I had just brushed my teeth, but apparently—as a number of kind readers assured me—this happens to lots of folks. However, I believe I hit a new low today when I emerged from the shower having shaved only one leg. It was not an aesthetically pleasing look, and not, I felt, a good sign.

Here's another sign of early senility: I'm having trouble retrieving the words I need. Just in the last few days, for example, I couldn't recall the word for "cul-de-sac" or "card table." I fear that my brain, in a desperate effort to maintain memory capacity, is alphabetically deleting words I don't use often, and we're already past the "c"s. As I say, not a good sign.

However, the most alarming thing that happened to me lately was what I have come to call The Case of the Missing Pants.

It began one day about 3 weeks ago, when I couldn't find my favorite pair of Eddie Bauer tan pants. I went through my closet probably 10 times, carefully sliding back each hanger, looking under the jackets, checking behind the enormous, Cinderella-style prom dress (my daughter's, not mine), but nothing. I even checked under the bed, behind the cedar chest, in the linen closet. More nothing. (Well, a lot of dust, but nothing wearable.)

Next, I did what I always do in such circumstances: I accused my husband of taking them. I mean by accident, of course—he doesn't have any particular fondness for women's chinos. We're simply the same height and own several pair of jeans and chinos that look similar.

And my husband does have a bad track record when it comes to mistakenly taking my clothing. When we were newlyweds, he mistook a pair of my favorite jeans for his and cut off the legs to make them into shorts. More recently, he threw out my best pair of khaki shorts. He thought they were his, couldn't figure out why he had bought something in such a girlie style, and tossed them. Neither of these incidents is remembered as a happy moment in our marriage.

So, clearly, I had good reason to suspect the man; however, a careful search of his side of the closet and his dresser drawers (not to mention the wastebasket) turned up nothing.

Naturally, I checked with my daughters, too. I accused my older daughter of accidentally having transported them to college in a basket of clean laundry. But no, she assured me, my tan chinos are nothing she would ever mistake for hers. (Take that, Mom.) For a while, I held out hope that an archaeological dig through the layers of clothes on my younger daughter's bedroom floor might unearth something. It didn't—though we found some good Easter candy, so it wasn't a complete waste.

While all this was going on, I racked my brain trying to recall when I had last worn the pants. I thought I had worn them when my family took me to dinner on Mother's Day. But then, where did they go? I was pretty sure I hadn't taken them off in the restaurant. I mean, I had a glass of wine with dinner, but just one.

"I'm sure I was wearing pants when we got home," I joked to my older daughter. She gave me one of those "That's not funny" looks that told me that, although she is now a recent college graduate herself, she is not yet ready to hear stories of my college days.

As the weeks went by, I remained confident that these favorite tan chinos would emerge someday, somewhere. That is, until yesterday morning at 5 a.m., when I was gathering clothes from my closet to wear to work. That's when I had it: the most bizarre—and yes, fairly alarming—epiphany of my life.

I realized I didn't own a pair of Eddie Bauer tan chinos. I had, in fact, never owned one.

Before you start avoiding me in the street, let me quickly add, in my defense, that I do own a pair of *black* Eddie Bauer chinos, as well a *chocolate brown* pair; unfortunately, just nothing answering to that description in tan. Of course, I acknowledge that this makes it rather unlikely that those particular tan pants had ever been my favorite.

"Well," said my husband, speaking slowly and eyeing me a little warily, "that certainly explains why you couldn't find them."

What can I say? I now fear that my brain has deleted words all the way through the letter "s," because clearly, "sanity" is already gone.

Remind Me Again Why I'm Writing This?

The people at my bank are starting to recognize me. And not in a good sort of way.

When I walk through the door, I see them reach reflexively for the large binder that—although I've never seen its cover—I'm pretty sure is labeled "Idiots who drive off and leave their cards in the ATM machine."

Okay, maybe that's not exactly written on the cover, but it's got to be what they're thinking.

In my defense, I'd like to point out that drive-thru ATMs require a fair amount of physical coordination and mental focus. The combination of the two has never been my strong suit.

First, when you arrive at the ATM, you have to remember either to put the car in park or keep your foot on the brake at all times. Failure to do so will result in immediate loss of your place in line.

Second, these machines ask a lot of questions. I would like to be able to push a button that says, "I'll take the usual," but sadly, ATM machines have none of the qualities of a good bartender.

Finally, if you're trying to push all the buttons at the same time you're listening to a climactic scene in an audiobook or explaining to your daughter how you don't understand the new Lady Gaga song, something crucial is bound to be lost.

Frankly, I think it's impressive that anyone can emerge from a drive-thru ATM with the correct amount of cash, a receipt, their bank card, and their side-view mirror still attached. Clearly, I can't.

By now, I have the ritual down for recovering a lost ATM card. I go to the bank after 2 p.m., when they empty the machine, produce some ID, sign the notebook, and they give me back my card. On the scale of humiliations I regularly endure, this is not a particularly bad one. Still, I secretly fear they have my photo taped under the counter with the caption "Repeat Offender" and the hand-written admonition, "No lollipop."

I will admit, however, that ATM machines are not at the root of my problem. What concerns me is my general level of "spaciness," which has been on the rise lately. I seem to be having issues with short-term memory.

My friends assure me that my forgetfulness has nothing to do with early senility. "You just have too much on your mind," they say. Or, "you're too busy; you can't keep track of everything."

I'd like to believe them…And yet, when I started that sentence, it had an ending. See what I mean?

It's not bad enough that I stare at the vitamin bottle each morning and wonder, "Did I just take a vitamin?" Or that I've been known to check whether the soap in the soapdish is wet to determine whether I've already washed my face. Yesterday, I added a new lapse to my repertoire. I was getting out of the shower when I realized I couldn't recall whether I had washed my hair.

I touched my hair to check for clues. It was wet, of course, but then again, I had just been in the shower. I would have been a little suspicious if it hadn't been wet. I picked up the shampoo bottle. It also was wet. But as it, too, had been in the vicinity of a great deal of spraying water, this again seemed inconclusive.

In such situations, what can one do? I washed my hair again—or possibly for the first time. Who could say?

All I can conclude is that when your personal instant-replay button no longer functions, you'd better start paying more attention to the game.

Happily, I'm not alone in my short-term memory problems, which makes them seem more normal. I've noticed that my husband is having issues as well. For example, I recently watched as he brushed his teeth, put away the toothbrush, and one minute later brushed his teeth again.

He denied it vigorously, but I know what I saw. My problem is short-term memory, not hallucinations.

I think.

About the Author

Nancy Crochiere has been a writer and editor since roughly around the time the earth started to cool. While most of her working life has centered on the development of educational materials, she has written articles for magazines and newspapers, training materials for business, skits for church variety shows, and highly creative notes excusing her daughters for being tardy to school. She wrote a popular humor column, "The Mother Load," for *The Daily News of Newburyport*, Massachusetts, from 1997 to 2011; and from 2006-2008, the column also appeared in *The Eagle-Tribune* of North Andover, Massachusetts.

With the help of her husband, Paul, Nancy raised two daughters with some success, meaning that so far neither child has shown any inclination to knock over a convenience store. In her free hours, she is learning to speak Italian and can often be found at the gym, trying hard not to trip over her bench during step class. Nancy also adores drinking wine and occasionally discussing the assigned book with her women's book group. She will gladly discuss any vacation destination that involves the phrase "warm, tropical breeze." She lives in Amesbury, Massachusetts.